THE WORK SMARTER GUIDE FOR NEW MANAGERS

Maria Duthoit

Series Editor David Kean

ROBINSON

First published in Great Britain in 2025 by Robinson

10 9 8 7 6 5 4 3 2 1

Copyright © Maria Duthoit, 2025

The moral rights of the author have been asserted.

All rights reserved.

No part of this publication may be reproduced, stored in a retrieval system, or transmitted, in any form, or by any means, without the prior permission in writing of the publisher, nor be otherwise circulated in any form of binding or cover other than that in which it is published and without a similar condition including this condition being imposed on the subsequent purchaser.

A CIP catalogue record for this book is available from the British Library.

ISBN: 978-1-47215-015-8

Typeset in Sentinel and Scala Sans by Ian Hughes

Printed and bound in Great Britain by Clays Ltd, Elcograf S.p.A.

Papers used by Robinson are from well-managed forests and other responsible sources.

Robinson
An imprint of
Little, Brown Book Group
Carmelite House
50 Victoria Embankment
London EC4Y 0DZ

The authorised representative
in the EEA is
Hachette Ireland
8 Castlecourt Centre, Dublin 15, D15 YF6A, Ireland
(email: info@hbgi.ie)

An Hachette UK Company

www.hachette.co.uk
www.littlebrown.co.uk

Maria Duthoit has spent over twenty years helping people and businesses grow – as a business leader, coach and author. She first became a manager at twenty-three and has since led a wide range of teams – from frontline client service teams to senior project groups spanning multiple countries.

Maria spent nearly a decade at Google, where she led international sales teams managing some of the company's largest clients – delivering ambitious commercial results while building strong, human-centred partnerships. Before that, she spent a decade at global advertising agencies like BBDO, Leo Burnett and McCann Erickson, helping international brands grow in emerging markets.

Today, Maria is Managing Partner at Catalyst, where she supports leaders and their teams through executive coaching, training and commercial strategy. She is a certified coach and holds an Executive MBA from HEC Paris. Her work is grounded in a clear strategic lens and a deep understanding of people – helping teams reach the next level, leaders find their voice and organisations get unstuck. Maria cares deeply about women's leadership and supports female managers and executives, helping them overcome self-doubt and grow into confident, authentic leaders.

She is the author of *The Work Smarter Guide to Sales* (2024). This is her second book – written for anyone stepping into management, or still finding their footing in the role.

Also in this series
The Work Smarter Guide to Sales
The Work Smarter Guide to Presenting
The Work Smarter Guide to Negotiation
The Work Smarter Guide to Marketing
The Work Smarter Guide to Pitching

'This book is the perfect starting point for new managers. It gives you a clear view of the landscape – and helps focus on what matters most. With warmth and encouragement, it helps you become aware of your new role, understand yourself better and shine a light on the questions and challenges you hadn't yet seen. A thoughtful, motivating guide to moving from "I don't know what I don't know" to a place of curiosity, clarity and growth. Highly recommended'
Maxim Braverman, Managing Director at Google Middle East and Northern Africa

'A brilliant guide for your first steps into management – honest, practical and written with warmth and a light touch. Most of us learn to lead others the hard way. This book helps turn that first experience into a strong foundation to build on – not a painful lesson to recover from. What makes this book especially relatable is how the author weaves in her early experiences with gentle humour – offering real-life examples that stay with you. Grounded in real human dynamics and refreshingly free of generic leadership advice, it offers the clarity, tools and support I wish every new manager had'
Anastasia Mikhalina, Global Talent Acquisition Director at L'Oreal

'A practical playbook for new leaders. From "setting OKRs" to "addressing limiting beliefs", powerful frameworks that I personally discovered first-hand at Google and Meta over the years are reintroduced. And rightly so! Highly recommended'
Clement Schvartz, Country Managing Director Europe, Board Member at Pinterest

'"The brain is like a muscle," as Maria Duthoit accurately says, and her book is the perfect training programme for it. Read it and become the manager you'll enjoy being – and win!'
Benoit Cacheux, Global Chief Digital Officer at Zenith, Publicis Group

'I wish I had come across this book twenty years ago – when I first became a manager. It captures the key challenge of transitioning from expert to leader with clarity and depth. What makes it especially valuable is its holistic approach: it addresses not only the mindset shift but also offers a wealth of practical, down-to-earth tools for managing yourself and your team through this transition. This book helps avoid the common pitfalls of early leadership, inspiring a more conscious, thoughtful path into management. A truly timely and much-needed guide'
Evgeniya Brodskaya, Director of Ecosystem at Google

'If you start your managerial journey, this book is a must! You will find priceless advice, practical exercises, concrete examples, but also common mistakes and traps that may hold you back. It's well written, very easy to read and superbly helpful. Thank you, Maria Duthoit, for sharing your experience and your thoughts with generosity and grace'
Marc Beretta, Academic Director of Executive Programs, Affiliate Professor at HEC Paris, MCC (ICF), Certified Master Coach

'In a world full of leadership advice, this book gives new managers what they actually need: practical tools, clarity of vision and the courage to lead their own way'
David Ponzo, Chief Commercial Officer at Louis Vuitton

Dedication:

To my family: Pierric, Asya, Leo, Antoinette and Michelle. Thank you for being you.

Acknowledgements:

To the colleagues and friends who helped make this book possible – and who continue to inspire me every day: Yulia Anfilova, Max Braverman, David Kean, Tom Asker, Vlad Kirakosyan, Oussama Doudouh, Evgeniya Brodskaya, Jane Grigoreva, Motunrayo Olaogun, Alexandre Visage, Sergey Kharitonov, Jeanne Nicolay, Natalia Sellibara.

Contents

Introduction	1
Mission 1: Survive the identity crisis	5
Answer the question: Why am I here?	8
What resources do you currently have at hand and how can you use them wisely?	9
Make your life easier with OKR	12
Delegate and make time for what matters	16
Trade perfectionism for curiosity	19
Mission 2: Move feedback into the here and now	25
Fight, flight or freeze	25
The depth of 'encourage the good and discourage the bad'	29
Be predictable	31
THE difficult conversation	33
What if the feedback is about you?	37
Mission 3: Make growth your survival strategy	41
Removing the barriers to growth	44
Helping people grow	52
Motivation and incentives for growth	55
Growth needs a roadmap	60
Your team's strongest growth driver?	62

Mission 4: Turn your team into your biggest project   63
Hire people who raise the bar for you and for others   66
Hiring do's and don'ts   69
Letting people go – the cost of hesitation   78

Mission 5: Expand your playing field   83
System thinking   84
Strategic thinking   87
Political intelligence   91
The most common traps that hold you back   96

Epilogue   100
Index   102

Introduction

During World War II, American troops set up bases on Pacific islands, flying in humanitarian aid for the local population. Once the war ended, the aid programme was discontinued. The Americans left and the islanders never really understood whether they should expect more food and clothing. After waiting some time, they decided to take action: they built makeshift air traffic control towers, cleared runways and even built wooden aeroplanes. They reasoned that if they re-enacted everything that had preceded the arrival of the supplies, then the cargo would surely appear again.

Poor, naive islanders. When I was a young manager seeking my own path, this was the most valuable story I heard. The story illustrates 'cargo cult thinking' – the belief that performing certain rituals and recreating the conditions which led to something good happening in the past will generate the same results in the future.

Yet, this same way of thinking plays out every day in countless organisations around the world. Managers in large corporations follow scripts and formulas, consult corporate playbooks, hold meetings with their subordinates and fill out evaluation forms. Managers in small businesses copy the 'best practices' of big corporations, replicate strategies and tactics and introduce corporate jargon to make everything sound more important to their own teams. Then everyone waits for success to arrive! But, more often than not, it doesn't arrive, or what arrives is a partial win – a result good enough to feel safe, but far from what could have been achieved if boldness, clarity and intention had been put into action. A comfortably unimpressive result.

My own first day as a manager replicated cargo cult thinking exactly. I became a manager at twenty-three. On a Friday evening, my boss told me I was being promoted to group head. On Monday I met two friendly people from another department, looking at me with warm curiosity – my new team. That's when I froze: I had absolutely no idea what to talk about or what to ask but I quickly reasoned to myself that bosses usually organise meetings and give people tasks. So I immediately set up a team meeting. Of course, it turned out to be completely useless and chaotic, as I tried to ask questions and collect ideas, all while battling inner panic. My team began to give me strange looks. I was so stressed that I even mixed up their names at the end. A total disaster.

Imitating actions, trying to formally reproduce what's been observed, overheard or created before, is a perfectly natural human reaction in an unfamiliar and confusing situation. How many times have we all heard that often-quoted piece of advice, 'fake it till you make it'? Maybe sometimes that tactic does work. But definitely not in people management. To be fair, you can find cargo cult practitioners even in the highest echelons of corporate power. Occasionally, people manage to build quite a substantial career by continually encouraging their teams to build wooden planes and wait for success and recognition. But usually, it's perfectly obvious to those around them what they're doing, and such leaders go down in history as buzzword merchants.

So where do the origins of this behaviour lie? Simple. In most cases, new managers don't receive any training or support. Research by the Chartered Management Institute in 2023 showed that four out of five managers fall into this category. Left to sink or swim, new managers face high stress, limited time and no proper training – all of which inevitably leads to a poorly considered and superficial approach to their work. The best you can hope for is mediocrity of performance and a disappointed team. Crucially, it also causes the new manager to start disliking this most wonderful aspect of their job – managing people.

Often, new managers are former specialists who excelled in their field and loved what they did. Becoming a manager without any support or understanding of the true nature of this new role, they continue to love everything related to their specialist skills – where they feel most comfortable – and either dislike or avoid anything to do with the new people-management aspects of the role. In my coaching practice, I've often come across such avoidant behaviour: my clients admit that they're intimidated by difficult conversations, by the need to motivate people and by finding the time to fill in performance forms. (One of my clients even exclaimed in frustration, 'If only I could keep the same resources but outsource the team management part, my life would be so much better!')

I totally understand where they're coming from, but, I have to admit, it always makes me sad to hear statements like that. Over twenty years in management, I've experienced the full spectrum of emotions about this job. Yet I firmly believe that once you grasp its essence, you can find immense joy in it: the process itself, the fruits of working together and the way your team and you evolve through interacting with each other.

This book is for those who are now at the beginning of their managerial journey. There's an incredible amount of information around us that, in theory, could help a novice manager. Management and leadership are clearly at the top of the list when it comes to sheer variety of content: from inch-thick academic sociology papers to pithy quotations on leadership. But which part of it is going to help you step into a new role *right now*?

In this book, I've prepared five missions for you. Each one will help you figure out what's important and what's not so important, where your influence lies and what's better left to others; how to discover your inner 'anchors' – those principles and values that keep you grounded, and define a clear sense of purpose, for yourself and your team. We'll talk about owning the change from individual contributor to manager, handling difficult conversations, growing people, building a team and stepping up to a new level of complexity in the company. I've chosen these five areas because, throughout my career, I've seen them emerge again and again as critical for new managers. I've managed customer service teams in international advertising agencies like BBDO, Leo Burnett and McCann Erickson; spent a decade at Google leading multiple commercial teams across markets and industries; and worked as a coach with managers of all levels – from first-time team leads to senior leaders in global organisations. These missions reflect the patterns I've observed, the challenges I've faced myself, and the tools I've seen make a lasting difference.

As we go through these five missions, we'll discuss both WHAT matters and HOW to implement it, so you can think it all through and create *your own unique style*. I hope this book will be a good starting point for building your awareness as a leader and, possibly, be the beginning of your love affair with managing people.

MISSION 1:
Survive the identity crisis

From my experience, the hardest thing a new manager faces in the early days of their new role isn't the increased workload, the different tasks or even the new level of responsibility. Although all of these are undoubtedly significant changes in day-to-day work, the most difficult part is a *new understanding of oneself*. The familiar confidence – the one that came from feeling capable, respected, and fully in control in the expert role – fades, giving way to questions instead: Who am I now? What can I offer my team and the company as a whole? How can I once again feel like I'm standing firmly on my own two feet?

This period could quite fittingly be called a crisis of identity, and I often compare the feelings and experiences of a new manager to the metamorphosis of Alice in Lewis Carroll's story. Her dialogue with the Caterpillar captures the depth of her confusion:

> 'Who are you?' said the Caterpillar.
>
> This was not an encouraging opening for a conversation. Alice replied, rather shyly, 'I – I hardly know, sir, just at present – at least I know who I was when I got up this morning, but I think I must have been changed several times since then.'
>
> 'What do you mean by that?' said the Caterpillar sternly. 'Explain yourself!'
>
> 'I'm afraid I can't explain myself, sir,' said Alice, 'because I'm not myself, you see.'
>
> 'I don't see,' said the Caterpillar.

> *'I'm afraid I can't put it more clearly,' Alice replied very politely, 'for I can't understand it myself to begin with; and being so many different sizes in a day is very confusing.'*

This analogy first came to me while working with my client Anna, who described her feelings in a remarkably similar way. Although she had been leading a team of seven people for over a year, she still struggled to find her internal 'balance point'. She shared how her perception of herself could change drastically, even within a single day. While talking with her team or holding meetings as the head of the department, she felt like an important boss, a key decision-maker, as someone shaping destinies. Yet, the moment she attended a meeting with her own manager or joined a group session with senior leadership, she felt more like a little girl who had been placed in charge by mistake and was about to be exposed at any moment. Many people suffer from similar emotions – it's called 'imposter syndrome'.

The turning point that led her to seek coaching was some unexpected feedback she received from her manager during her annual review. At the end of their conversation, he said, 'Listen, I can see how much effort you're putting in. But you need to understand, there's no need to keep proving to everyone that you deserve this role. You're already in it, and that's a fact.'

However supportive the intent behind her manager's comment may have been, it didn't resolve the most critical question: how do you change your internal perspective? How do you transition from one state to another and feel firmly established in your new role?

No matter what kind of transition, transformation or adaptation we talk about, it's impossible to make the leap instantly by simply deciding to, or just by listening to a podcast on the subject. Psychologists have long studied how people adjust to new roles and identities. The research shows that change always happens in stages – some of them quite uncertain and uncomfortable – before you reach a sense of stability and confidence in your new role.

In my observation, not all new managers experience the transition as deeply or as reflectively as my client, Anna. Sometimes blind spots and insecurities are successfully masked by psychological defences – in which case all that surfaces is stress, discomfort or even a show of bravado: 'If I'm in this position now, it means I'm special, chosen – the smartest, and invulnerable.' Over time, though, this stance usually backfires. A lack of humility makes it hard to listen, and sooner or later, reality responds: a project fails, the team pushes back, or feedback from above is less glowing than expected. And when it does, the fall is much harder – because it wasn't just a mistake, it was a mistake made in complete confidence. Sometimes, though, there is no loud fall – just a slow slide into unawareness. The manager keeps copying what they think leadership looks like, convinced they're doing it right. Eventually, they become a lifelong follower of the 'cargo cult'.

If, like Anna, you feel lost and unsettled during this period, I urge you to treat yourself with patience and compassion – just as you would a close friend going through a challenging period of change.

One stage of the transformation follows another, and you need time to live through each of them: from the euphoria of promotion, to the crisis of realising the scale of the change, adapting to it and finding your own way. And finally, the stage of *settling in* to your new role. What's important is that every psychological model of transition describes the final point as a confident affirmation in the new state – which means a happy ending is inevitable.

Let's look at what significantly eases the transformation, making it more meaningful and conscious. Something that will help you become more proactive and influential in shaping your life, even during challenging times.

Over the years, I've seen what works – and what doesn't – both from my own experience and from working with new managers. Here are the points to help you get through those important first three to six months in your role. These first months are crucial. If you spend your time on the wrong things or you don't fully understand the core of your role, you'll create problems that only grow bigger with time.

Answer the question: Why am I here?

At first, your role might seem pretty straightforward – the title says it all, right? What could possibly be complex about the tasks of a Head of Sales, an Analytics Manager or a Customer Support Lead? And yet, reality is full of nuances – and it's your call to explore them all.

Job descriptions often just list tasks and duties but they rarely tell you the whole story: what's your team actually doing to help the organisation hit its main goals? How can this be measured? Which dimensions does this measurement include? Another, less broad but equally critical question, is this: what is expected of you right now, considering the current context in which your team operates? Perhaps your immediate task is to handle a crisis or to rebuild a close-knit team after mistakes made by a previous manager. The quicker you know, the better.

Start by talking to your own manager. What's expected of you? What does success actually look like? How precisely will your success be assessed, beyond the standard metrics? What is the biggest challenge of your role? How is your department perceived within the company?

If your manager hasn't clearly defined what they expect, treat this as a carte blanche – an opportunity to set your own goals, ones that are specific and easy to measure. Above all, I urge you: never agree to ambiguous goals or generalised statements.

Don't just rely on your boss's point of view. Talk to other people you'll be working with – you'll need those connections anyway. This includes not only people within the organisation but also external partners and clients. Use your position as the new person to ask all the basic 'stupid' questions. These questions, far from being trivial, are essential for uncovering the essence of things, identifying overlaps, blind spots and opportunities. Think of it as creating a map of the territory based on other people's views. To make this map as accurate and comprehensive as possible, you'll need to speak with as many individuals as you can, each offering a different perspective.

Why bother having all these conversations? Because no presentation or job description will ever tell you what you really need to know.

Talking to people is the only way to figure out what vague phrases like 'unlock potential' or 'create synergy' actually mean. As Theodor W. Adorno put it, 'Vague expression permits the hearer to imagine whatever suits him and what he already thinks in any case.' When such an attitude multiplies across an organisation, the resulting collaboration can end up feeling like everyone's busy, but no one knows what's actually going on. To get to the heart of things, you'll need to think like a detective: talk to people, check the facts and connect the dots.

We often adopt corporate jargon without realising it. To make sure you truly understand the context and your goals, there's a funny exercise you can try: explain the essence of your role in a way that your grandmother would understand. It actually forces you to translate corporate language into human terms. If you don't have a curious grandmother or a ten-year-old child at hand to ask you questions like 'Why?' or 'What does that mean?' or 'What's it for?', try the exercise with an imagined audience or with a generative AI tool like ChatGPT. Ask it to help you ensure that there's no trace of corporate jargon or ambiguity in your description of your job.

What resources do you currently have at hand and how can you use them wisely?

One of history's most striking examples of catastrophically poor planning is Napoleon's invasion of Russia. His army became bogged down in the snow near Moscow and was forced to turn back due to the cold and exhaustion. No one wishes to find themselves in such a miserable and foolish situation (though, admittedly, it was quite fortunate for the opposing side). This is why it is vital to take a close look at your aims and the resources available to you right now: your team; the time you have to deliver on your plans; your budgets; external and internal partners; technical resources – the list can continue or change depending on your industry and the size of your business.

Although all these elements are exceptionally important when assessing your overall situation, in this book we shall focus on your most crucial resource – your team. The reality is, your success entirely depends on your ability to get the right people and turn them into a proper team.

In your new role, your results are no longer just about you; they're about what you and your people accomplish *together*. Or, to cut to the heart of it: in the eyes of your company and your clients, you *are* your team.

There can be no compromise when it comes to your team. That is precisely why I suggest keeping a clear, ideal vision of what it should be, and working towards making that vision a reality as quickly as possible. At this early stage, it means starting with an honest look at where you stand. You won't have all the answers yet – but this initial assessment will help you begin to see the shape of the team you're working with.

What does this mean in practical terms? You need to evaluate:

- Whether the size and composition of the team truly match your objectives. Perhaps, instead of five salespeople and one analyst, you might need one salesperson and five analysts.
- How competent and experienced they are; who is a key player and who is a novice. Who can you entrust with significant tasks and who will require training and support?
- How motivated your people are and how satisfied they are with their work. What are their strengths and weaknesses? With

whom can you forge long-term plans and with whom might you need to part ways?
- How the team functions on a day-to-day basis. Does everyone work together seamlessly, as though they understand each other without speaking or do they keep rubbing each other up the wrong way?
- How your team collaborates with other departments and external partners or clients. How are they perceived as a group and how is each individual viewed from the outside?

When examining the people in your team, I urge you to be as impartial as possible – take the role of an observer and refrain from jumping to hasty conclusions, whether negative or positive. Your first impressions and the initial information you receive can be misleading; in time, your understanding of these individuals' capabilities and how they can contribute within the team may shift dramatically.

If you are beginning to lead your peers, do your best to avoid the trap of bias – good or bad – that may stem from your preconceptions. Often, the people with whom you most enjoy exchanging the day's news or gossip over a pint after work are not the best experts at their jobs, while those who might have occasionally said 'no' to you could be the ones who know how to prioritise their responsibilities.

If you are entirely new to the company, be prepared for unexpected twists. My friend Guillaume, for example, found himself responsible for six people: three pairs of sales managers, each pair working in its own client sector. Two of these pairs were flourishing, with steady revenue growth and ambitious plans, while the third pair was not exactly failing but its growth had flatlined. Guillaume spent a considerable amount of time trying to find out what was holding back the business. He delved into market figures, studied the client offering and scrutinised competitors' products – all of which were perfectly rational steps. However, as he eventually discovered, the primary obstacle to growth was right under his nose: a conflict within the team itself. Competition between the two managers in the third pair had intensified far too much, and their dissatisfaction had begun to surface in highly unpleasant ways. They argued over whose clients took priority; one would fail to show up at the other's 'client day' at the last moment, sabotaging a presentation; and disputes over resources with partner teams could escalate into a serious issue. Naturally, all of this stood in the way of business growth. Guillaume had to reorganise his entire team and dismiss one of the clashing managers, as that person was unwilling to abandon his own entitled attitude. Some might say Guillaume did not spend enough time resolving the conflict or boosting motivation, but for him, eliminating toxicity quickly and aiming for strong team performance took priority.

This story isn't just about how team dynamics rather than any outside business issue can have the biggest impact on results. The real issue was that neither the team nor their partner departments had a clear understanding of their true priorities – which only made the conflict worse. There were no clear agreements about objectives in place.

When goals and objectives aren't clearly defined – or are left vague and open to interpretation – things fall apart. Teams lose alignment, conflicts arise over priorities and resources, and before long, you hear sarcastic remarks by the coffee machine: 'What on earth do they even do in that team?' The only real fix for this is to bring in the OKR (Objectives and Key Results) system.

Make your life easier with OKR

OKR (Objectives and Key Results) are very well known in the business world. Indeed, most people would agree that setting the right goals and defining clear, measurable outcomes is both good and necessary. Yet, from what I've seen, despite their growing popularity and frequent adoption in new organisations, very few people actually use OKRs properly – or get the most out of them. OKR International, a management consultancy, reported some rather telling figures: according to their research, in 2023, 78 per cent of respondents admitted they did not get OKRs right when the system was first introduced in their company. My guess is that many never really engage with the system at all: they either abandon it if no one keeps an eye on the process, or they fill in their OKRs as a mere formality. That's a shameful waste of a very useful tool.

I once spent quite a bit of time getting my team (and, I'll admit, myself too) into the habit of using OKRs. When OKRs were first introduced across the organisation, my sales managers – already swamped with work – saw the whole process of carefully setting goals and outcomes as a waste of valuable time. Time they'd much rather spend on something useful, like meeting clients.

So I suggested we try it properly for just one quarter. I said, 'Let's not do this for the sake of compliance – let's do it for ourselves. Let's see if it can actually make our lives easier.' And it did. Not only did it make all our efforts clearer and more focused, it also brought an unexpected benefit – it made it easier for us to say no. That was the first real advantage we felt: finally being able to turn down colleagues who kept showing up with 'urgent' tasks (urgent for them, not for us). In Google's friendly culture, saying no wasn't easy. Yet once we had OKRs written down and agreed, they became a sort of final word – there was no point in challenging them or trying to argue.

We won't go into every detail of the OKR system here but there are a few key points worth noting. First and foremost, as I've already mentioned, OKRs are a way to get everyone – yourself, your team and those around you – on the same page about what really matters and what doesn't. What needs to start happening and what needs to stop.

The most important test of a good OKR is whether the goals you've set match the company's biggest priorities right now.

Keep in mind that OKRs aren't meant to list everything you do at work. They're not a to-do list, nor an endless exercise in writing down your responsibilities. Think of them instead as the missing links that turn broad strategy into clear, measurable steps that actually get done.

In this simple abbreviation:

O (Objective) sets the direction – it's an ambitious but realistic goal, written in a way that makes sense not just to your team but to other departments (and even to the infamous grandmother from our earlier test).

KR (Key Results) define the outcomes – clearly stated, measurable, and tied to a deadline. A result can't be vague, subjective or open to interpretation. What does *'strong performance'* or *'a clear success'* actually mean without specifics? At the end of the set period, you should be able to answer with a simple *yes* or *no* – was the result achieved or not?

Here's a fictional example and a short checklist to help you get started. What's the real test for any OKR? Check if it can be more concise and precise?

Objective:
Make our customer support the #1 rated in the industry.

Checklist:
- *Is it aspirational, creating a clear 'before and after'? Yes*
- *Is it concise? Yes*
- *Is it clear, providing a picture of the desired outcome? Yes*
- *Does it contribute to the overall strategic goal? Yes*

Key results:
1. Reduce response time to under X minutes while keeping first-

contact resolution at Y per cent, making us the fastest in the industry – by Q3.
2. Increase 5-star ratings on post-interaction surveys from A per cent to B per cent through real-time coaching and quality reviews for support agents – by Q4.
3. Launch an AI chatbot by Q2 to handle Z per cent of queries, so agents can focus on complex cases – by Q4.

Checklist:
- *Are they measurable, with clear 'yes' or 'no' results? Yes*
- *Are they time-bound? Yes*
- *Are they challenging but realistic? Yes*
- *Are they objective and free of subjective criteria? Yes*
- *Are they directly connected to the objective and the wider strategic goal? Yes*

Ideally, OKRs should work at every level – from the company's overall strategy down to each individual's personal goals. And yes, your own OKRs could even include learning Mongolian, if that's not just a personal passion but genuinely useful for achieving key company objectives.

For OKRs to be motivating, team OKRs should be set by the manager and agreed with the team, while individual OKRs must be written by the individual themselves. One of my coaching clients once complained during a session that her team kept resisting the OKRs she had written for each of them, always finding reasons not to follow through. Hardly surprising – no one likes being told what to do.

Trying to set personal tasks for your team might seem like care and attention but more often than not, it's just a poorly disguised need for control. And that same urge to keep everything under tight supervision is exactly what stops many new managers from (truly) learning how to delegate.

Delegate and make time for what matters

There are only two real reasons why new managers hesitate to delegate tasks: fear of mistakes and the urge to stay in control.

One of my team members, newly promoted to a managerial role, once told me that delegating felt like handing over your baby to strangers and hoping they wouldn't drop it. A rather anxious feeling indeed!

And yet, the ability to delegate wisely and with confidence is what separates a manager who has made it through the identity crisis from someone who still behaves like an expert who has been asked to keep an eye on the team for a while.

I've often seen new managers look for reasons why delegation is simply impossible – they usually blame others. After all, it's easier just to do everything yourself. My friend Sam once shared a story with me: *'When I joined this new company, I assumed my team would just know what to do. The tasks seemed straightforward and they'd been here ages, so I figured they'd just crack on. I'd say, "We need to cut the marketing budget," expecting them to know exactly what to do. But things kept slipping and I couldn't get my head around why. I'd be sitting there thinking, "Why isn't this getting sorted? Is it them, or is it me?" Eventually, I realised – I wasn't giving enough context or making it clear what I actually wanted. I was just chucking the ball over the fence and hoping for the best.'*

It's true – others can't read your mind. And if you don't take the time to clearly agree on what's expected as the final result (which, once again, brings us back to OKRs), there's a high chance you'll end up disappointed with your team's work.

To be fair, full delegation isn't always the right approach. There are a few key conditions that make it a sensible and productive step:

- Team members have the necessary competence
- They take full responsibility for their work and projects
- They can collaborate effectively with colleagues, as well as with internal and external partners

You can only delegate with no sleepless nights when these three conditions are met. If they aren't – or not fully – there's still work to do. However, chances are your team includes a mix of experienced and less experienced members. You can always start by entrusting tasks to more seasoned ones, while offering extra support to those who need it.

Not all delegation works the same way. The right approach depends on both the person and the situation. Here are four main ways to do it:

- Directive style – in one sentence: 'Do as I say'.

When to use it: in emergencies, when working with new, inexperienced or struggling team members or when a task is urgent, critical or requires absolute precision.

- Collaborative style – in one sentence: 'Let's find a solution together'.

When to use it: when involving others will improve the outcome and lead to better ideas.

- Visionary style – in one sentence: 'Follow me'.

When to use it: when the goal is ambitious, demanding or requires real commitment. This works best for open-ended challenges that need creativity and motivation.

- Coaching style – in one sentence: 'You take the lead, and I'll guide you'.

When to use it: when the focus is on developing skills and helping someone grow into a role.

There's no such thing as a good or bad delegation style – each has its strengths and drawbacks and each has the right and wrong time to use it. Sticking to just one approach, even if it feels comfortable, can have unintended consequences.

A former colleague of mine was a firm believer in the coaching approach – which, without a doubt, is a valuable and effective way to work with people. However, over time, anonymous feedback in her management reviews started to sound negative: *'It feels like our manager avoids making decisions'* or *'She never gives a clear opinion – she just asks what we think'*.

And as for an overly directive style – well, I'm sure we've all got a story about that. No one likes a manager who just barks orders without paying attention to the people around them.

So, the real skill isn't about finding *your* one perfect delegation style – it's about having a range of approaches and choosing the right one for the moment. Just like picking the right outfit for the occasion, while still being yourself.

And of course, one of the biggest benefits of delegation is that it gives you back time to focus on *what truly matters*. It lets you step back and think – about where your team is heading, how to work better with other departments and what needs improving – all the things that new managers often don't have time for. (Mostly because their days are packed with firefighting or routine tasks.)

What do you call someone who delegates but still watches over their team's every move, double-checking the smallest details? That's right – the infamous micromanager.

No one wants to be seen as a micromanager. It's the opposite of being someone who focuses on what truly matters. Yet so many managers fall into this trap, driven by a fear of mistakes and a need for control – often without even noticing.

In my experience, I've seen all shades of micromanagement. After stepping into the role, many managers insist on being copied into every single email 'just to stay in the loop'. Others spend hours reworking the format of client proposals – changing fonts, tweaking headlines, adjusting spacing – while more urgent matters wait. One ex-colleague of mine asked his team for end-of-day breakdowns of how every hour was spent. This was on top of the agency timesheets they were already filling in! Another manager I knew drowned his team in reports and dashboards, unsure what he actually wanted to learn from the numbers.

And then there's my personal favourite: the manager who wanted to join every single client call. When two happened at the same time, she asked the team to record the Zoom so she could catch up on the one she'd missed – after work.

All of them had one thing in common: they were too busy managing the small stuff to focus on what actually matters. To sum it up, the pattern looks like this: fear of making a mistake → stress → the urge to control everything → micromanagement → no room for truly important, strategic work.

The moment you make a conscious decision to take the leap and start delegating, your life will get easier – even with the inevitable hiccups along the way. The most valuable of all resources will suddenly become available to you: time.

But it's vital to protect that time and use it wisely. For example, block out your mornings in the calendar – when your mind is still fresh and sharp – and dedicate them to thinking, planning and strategic work.

Speaking of managing time, we can't ignore burnout. For a new manager, it's a real risk – considering the stress, the heavy workload and the completely changed role. That's why I encourage you not just to set aside your mornings for reflection but also to build a few simple yet effective habits: leave your phone behind when you take a lunch break, make a firm decision not to check work emails at the weekend and make time for exercise.

Your brain will function far better if you give it proper rest. And if this sounds like just another piece of well-meaning advice, look up 'karoshi syndrome' – it might be a good enough reason not to test how long you can go without sleep or breaks.

Trade perfectionism for curiosity

In the music industry, there's a term: the 'difficult second album'. It describes the challenge artists face when creating a follow-up to a successful debut – expectations are sky-high, the pressure is intense and the fear of failure is overwhelming.

New managers often find themselves in a similar trap. You proved yourself as a great specialist, earned the trust of your company and were given a team along with bigger responsibilities. Now it feels as though failure is not an option. In fact, the stakes are even higher – you need to prove yourself all over again but this time, do even better.

It's an unsettling place to be. If fear of mistakes and the need to be perfect dictate your actions, they will hold you back. They will shape how you think, limit the solutions you come up with, influence how you work with your team and even affect how you manage upwards.

A common strategy is perfectionism. You become fixated on getting everything right, avoiding mistakes at all costs and always having the correct answers.

In my coaching practice, I've worked with many managers (and I must admit, most of them were women) who built an image in their minds of a flawless version of themselves – an ideal they felt they had to live up to. And worse, they constantly measured themselves against this ideal. But this version of themselves was vague, undefined and ultimately unattainable – like the horizon, always just out of reach. This mindset drains energy, fuels self-doubt and makes leadership far harder than it needs to be.

This approach exhausts the manager and makes the team suffer too – perfectionism demands endless effort and never allows anything to feel truly 'good enough'.

I can't simply tell you to stop worrying, let go of all your defences and instantly become self-aware and composed. That kind of shift takes time – and real effort – to develop a conscious, unbiased observer's perspective. But what I can offer is a different way of looking at things:

a mindset that can help you move forward by redirecting your focus and changing the way you approach your actions.

Embrace *proactive curiosity*. What do I mean by that? First and foremost, it's about shifting your focus towards investigation and exploration. You're in a new role, surrounded by new information, new interactions, new connections and new meanings – all this is true even if your promotion hasn't taken you beyond your department. Don't rush to draw conclusions, have all the answers or defend your position too soon.

You might argue that if you only ask questions and observe, you'll come across as passive or even a waste of people's time. And that's a fair point.

That's why curiosity alone isn't enough – it needs an active element. It's not just about gathering information and showing interest; it's about engaging with what you learn. Take what you see, filter it through your experience, your expertise, and your sound judgement, and make sense of it.

In other words, connect the dots. Spot patterns, uncover links and draw out new insights. It's these new insights that make up your real contribution.

It's hard to overstate the value of keen judgement. It allows leaders to see the structure and core of a situation – and to bring fresh perspective and new meaning to the status quo, which is exactly what the best leaders excel at.

One of my coaching clients, Linda, once came to a session with a long list of skills she believed she needed to develop in order to move up the career ladder. But when I asked her to think of a leader she had worked with – someone she truly admired and found inspiring – she immediately named a senior manager from a different function. According to Linda, this woman was highly respected in the company because she came up with fresh, strategically strong solutions to problems that seemed impossible to solve. But what struck Linda most was how she approached them. Before offering ideas, she would always start by asking the most basic, almost naive questions – openly admitting that she didn't know the specifics and wanted to get to the heart of the issue. And she did this without any fear of looking incompetent. During that session, Linda suddenly exclaimed in surprise, 'I have so many skills on my list, but what I really need to develop first is my keen judgement!'

If we're talking about the fresh perspectives and insights you can bring to those around you, it's not only about keen judgement. Your expertise and natural strengths – the very qualities that led to your promotion – matter just as much.

Think about it: why is it you who's doing this job now? Whether you've stepped into an existing team or are forming a new one, there's a reason you've been put in charge. What do you already do well that you can bring to your team right now?

Of course, this will evolve with time and experience. But even now, you have something valuable to offer. If, for example, you're particularly good at turning complexity into clarity, that's something you can start using straight away. Work it into your conversations, your explanations and your decision-making – it will make a difference from day one.

My former colleague Sarah, now a highly experienced and senior manager, started her career in a consulting firm. One of her greatest strengths was her natural sense of structure – she had a sharp, logical way of thinking and could communicate ideas clearly, always moving from the big picture to the finer details. But at the time, she didn't see it that way. She thought her main skill was simply making slides – which, to be fair, was a natural byproduct of her structured thinking. So, when she first became a manager, she spent much of her time tweaking and correcting slides for her team. The turning point came when one of her team members approached her, asking her to approve the colours and layout of some charts for a client presentation, reassuring her that everything else was already done. 'Surely I'm not here just to pick chart colours,' she thought to herself.

Let's be honest – getting everything absolutely right or perfect, especially from the start, is nearly impossible. Sure, it can happen, but more as a lucky outcome than something you can plan for. That's why it's so important to give yourself permission – genuinely – to be someone who tries, makes mistakes and finds their own way. This mindset builds self-trust, steadiness and, just as importantly, makes you more relatable to those around you.

This is what we call humility.

MISSION 2:

Move feedback into the here and now

I often hear from my clients – especially those new to management – that feedback conversations are one of the trickiest parts of the job. They call them 'difficult conversations', sigh, and glance away. And straight away, it's obvious – if merely talking about feedback makes them uncomfortable, actually giving it must feel much worse.

No wonder. Feedback isn't a message you just send and forget – it's a two-way exchange. There's always a chance of uncomfortable questions, pushback, or criticism of your decisions, not to mention an emotional reaction from the other person or even outright rejection of what you're saying. For a new manager, still going through an identity crisis and not yet fully comfortable in their role, this can feel incredibly stressful.

How do we react to this kind of stress? When faced with the tension and pressure of a difficult conversation, our brain falls into one of three instinctive responses: fight, flight or freeze. Of course, we don't choose these reactions consciously – they kick in under the influence of fear or the need to protect ourselves and save face.

Fight, flight or freeze

The first response, *fight*, promises a sense of safety and control – as long as you establish dominance and make sure the other person backs down. For new managers, this often comes out as: *'They're all lazy and irresponsible – why is it always down to me to sort everything out?'* Once someone locks into this mindset, they start twisting everything to fit that belief, no longer seeing things as they really are. And the trouble is, some managers never grow out of it – they carry this way of thinking with them throughout their careers.

I once spoke to a senior executive at a party who was complaining that he just couldn't find a decent second-in-command – someone who could 'knock some sense into all those dim-witted, incompetent people on my team. I'm sick of shouting at them and fighting all the time.' Listening to him, I felt a chill run through me. He was in charge of at least five hundred people around the world – and he thought they were *all* fools? A grim reality for everyone involved, including that yet-to-be-hired deputy, who was bound to get the same treatment.

The second response, *flight*, tempts us with the thought that if we ignore a problem for long enough, it might just go away on its own. Unsure how to handle the conversation, reluctant to dig too deep and wary of both their own emotions and those of others, a new manager may simply start avoiding feedback altogether. Instead, they pin their hopes on the annual performance review – a far safer bet. The timing will be right, the format already set, and the whole thing will feel much more structured and controlled. Much easier than dealing with it straight away. And in the meantime, they comfort themselves with the same thought as Scarlett O'Hara in *Gone with the Wind*: *'I'll think about it tomorrow!'*

The third response, *freeze*, is all about keeping the peace. Play it safe, keep everyone happy, don't rock the boat – that's the logic. Managers who fall into this pattern put their team's comfort above everything else. In coaching sessions, they often smile enthusiastically and say, *'I'm here to make my team happy!'* Their feedback is usually full of compliments and words of encouragement – which does have value, but only when it's grounded in something real and specific, rather than just hollow praise. These managers, often deeply empathetic and highly attuned to others, worry about hurting people with their words. In our sessions, we work together to challenge the idea that they are responsible for their team's happiness and to explore a different perspective: helping people step out of their comfort zone is also a way of caring about them, just in a different form.

MISSION 2: MOVE FEEDBACK INTO THE HERE AND NOW

Regardless of which avoidance strategy a manager follows, the outcome is often the same – in many companies, the annual performance review ends up being treated as the only real feedback conversation. For the team, the build-up to this meeting is often even more nerve-wracking than it is for the manager. They have no idea what to expect and can only guess. And those guesses are often way off: *'What if this conversation goes badly ... or maybe it won't? Will they praise me for that great project in May? Or will they only remember that tricky situation with my client in September? Will they recognise the long hours I put in? Or will all the good be overshadowed by that one (well, maybe more than one) mistake?'*

Feedback belongs in the here and now – its focus is on the present rather than the past. But instead of dwelling on what went wrong (or right) weeks or months ago, it should become a conversation about what can be done differently in the future – one you can approach with confidence and enthusiasm.

And once feedback is part of the present, there's no reason to turn it into a big occasion. The more weight you give it, the more it starts to feel like a high-stakes conversation – something both sides might find uncomfortable. But feedback isn't meant to be an ordeal; it should be as natural as anything else in your working life. We'll get into how to handle those conversations – including the difficult ones – later in the chapter.

We could stop there and say that's what one-to-ones and team debriefs are for. But in reality, it goes beyond that. What if I told you that every single interaction you have with your team – every single one – is either feedback or a task you're giving them?

I fully realised this after experiencing something first-hand that changed the way I dealt with my team – and with people in general. At the time, I was leading a sales team of eight. One day, in an internal meeting, we were discussing our plan of attack for one of our client sectors – what we could do to drive significant growth. The approach we developed relied heavily on data our analyst was meant to gather and process. Yet during the meeting, he seemed completely out of it. So afterwards, I deliberately passed by his desk and said something like, *'Cheer up, we're counting on you!'* Dan – that was his name – gave me a look as if he wanted to say something, but I was already turning away, rushing to my next meeting.

Two weeks later, we gave our presentation to the client, and it was a huge success. Barely two days later Dan ended up in hospital, completely burnt out. Later, he told me that at the time he had been struggling with the grief of losing his dog – a loss he blamed himself for. And then came my comment – blunt and straight to the point – calling him out on his attitude and reminding him the whole team was relying on him. That was all it took to push him over the edge, making him work past his limits, refusing to slow down. And in the end, it took a heavy toll.

When he told me, a heavy weight settled on me. He had been pushing himself too hard, convinced that anything less meant letting the team down. And I hadn't even noticed.

That was a lesson I wouldn't forget: every interaction with your team – no matter how small or fleeting – is either feedback or a task, and it needs to be taken seriously. Because it has consequences in their lives.

And it's not just about what you say. We don't always realise it, but everything we do sends a signal. A raised eyebrow, a sarcastic remark, a so-called *harmless* joke at someone's expense – or, on the flip side, a pat on the back, a kind word, even a genuine smile. That's all feedback too.

Even silence, even the absence of any reaction at all – people pick up on that. And it speaks volumes. All of these little moments add up. They shape your relationship with your team, whether it's in a one-to-one, a team meeting or just a passing chat by the coffee machine. It all matters.

Why do our words and reactions matter so much? Humans are social creatures. Throughout our lives, the people around us shape how we see and understand ourselves. But not everyone has the same impact – some figures hold far greater significance. Parents, teachers, friends, coaches and those we respect in our fields don't just influence our thinking – they help define our sense of self.

Of course, managers are part of this group too. More than that, we often – without even realising it – subconsciously assign them parental roles. That's simply how the human mind works. So when you step into a management role, you take on more than formal authority – you also inherit a certain invisible psychological power. And that's something to be aware of. It's not there to be wielded, and it's certainly not something to be taken advantage of.

The depth of 'encourage the good and discourage the bad'

There's really just one simple rule when it comes to feedback – and to building good relationships in general: encourage the good and discourage the bad. It's an idea most people have heard of, but it's often seen in a rather shallow and limited way. At its simplest, it sounds like *'praise what's right and ignore what isn't'* – which, if you don't look deeper, can end up as a hollow phrase.

Let's start with what it means to encourage the good. One of the most valuable things a manager can offer their team is genuine recognition and support. When my clients, friends, or colleagues talk about the best managers they've worked with, they almost always mention two things: (i) these managers understood their people and evidently believed in them, and (ii) they gave them the push they needed in order to grow – even when it meant stepping out of their comfort zone.

What's striking is how long that recognition stays with people. Years later, they still remember the exact words their manager said. So don't hold back – there's no sense in thinking, *If everything's fine, there's nothing to say.* 'When you acknowledge someone's efforts, avoid empty, general praise – it does little good. Recognition should be *specific and meaningful*; only then does it truly make a difference.

And don't just highlight clear-cut achievements. Pay attention to dedication, curiosity, kindness towards others, sound judgement, enthusiasm for big ideas, openness, honesty – anything that deserves to be seen and valued. These are just as important as results, and when people feel recognised for who they are – not just for what they deliver – it gives them confidence to grow.

I also want to warn you about undermining good behaviour – when someone puts in real effort and does something well, only to be met with indifference or even a negative response. Even if your reaction has nothing to do with their work, it still sends a message.

Imagine this: a team member spends time crafting an excellent report for a client and sends it over, expecting some kind of recognition. But instead of acknowledging their effort, your first response is to point out minor wording issues – or worse, you just fire off a dry *'Ok'* and immediately move on to another topic, launching into a barrage of questions. This kind of reaction, especially if it happens often, is one of the quickest ways to kill motivation and confidence. The person starts thinking that no matter how much effort they put in, it will either go unnoticed or be picked apart. And after a while, they stop bothering.

When it comes to discouraging the wrong behaviours, the details matter just as much. The key is staying calm and measured, taking the time to understand the situation, see the bigger picture and ask questions rather than jumping to conclusions. The aim isn't to shame someone for what's already happened – you can't change the past. It's about shifting the focus to the future: what can be learned from this, and what needs to change to stop it from happening again?

This might seem counterintuitive, but sometimes managers actually encourage the wrong behaviours without realising it. How? By letting them slide. For example, there's a big deadline coming up, and the manager avoids addressing a team member's lack of effort because they're worried about damaging morale. Or they're so impressed by someone's strengths that they turn a blind eye to their mistakes – convincing themselves that, surely, this person wouldn't get things wrong.

Before we get to the approach I recommend for giving corrective feedback – or, simply put, having a difficult conversation – there's one more important point to touch on. It's about communication in general.

Be predictable

Some people think predictability is a flaw – something dull, uninspiring, maybe even a bit rigid. But in reality, it's one of the strongest building blocks of good relationships. When people know what to expect from you (in a good way, ideally!), they feel at ease, more open, and able to concentrate on what really matters at work.

If you and your team agree from the start on what success looks like, there's far less room for misunderstandings or frustration. OKRs, which we touched on in Mission 1, are a great way to get that clarity early on – so there are no vague expectations or confusing performance standards. One of my coaching clients, Steve, once shared his frustration about working with his manager. Every time they discussed his progress, she would pick apart his work, but each time with a different set of expectations. 'At some point, I just gave up trying to figure out what she wanted,' Steve told me. 'I know she means well, but every time I try to push back or remind her of what we'd agreed, she moves the goalposts again. Honestly, I've stopped arguing – I just nod along. I feel like an idiot.'

Beyond the Key Results in your team's OKRs, it makes sense to agree on other important expectations too. Where is there room for creativity, and where should the team stick to the agreed process? When does speed matter more than quality? Which decisions can they make on their own, and when should they check with you first? When they want to reach out, should they email you, message you, book a meeting or just come over for a quick chat? If you don't discuss these things upfront, misunderstandings, frustration and disappointment are bound to happen.

Your emotional reactions should be predictable too. Stress can have a huge impact on how we interact with others – and even how we come across. Some people start talking too much and rushing around, others become short-tempered and irritable, while some withdraw completely and seem distant or cold. Our reactions under stress can be unpredictable and even hurtful – not just to those around us, who might take them personally, but to ourselves too. We're often not fully aware of how we come across.

The Hogan test – designed to reveal typical stress responses – became, for me, the answer to many questions about how I interacted with my team. My results showed that my instinctive reaction under heavy stress was to throw myself into problem-solving, shutting everything else out. To those around me, I came across as cold and distant – quite unlike my usual self, as I'm generally warm and fully engaged with others. But what made it even more jarring was how I responded to people who interrupted me in the middle of this intense focus. Since, in my mind, I was in the middle of *saving the world*, any distraction could trigger an unmistakable flicker of irritation. For colleagues used to my warmth – and completely unaware of what was going on in my head – it must have felt like being drenched with a bucket of cold water. This was a huge revelation. I'd noticed certain reactions from my team before, but I hadn't fully grasped how I must have appeared to them. Or how unpredictable my behaviour seemed.

Once I recognised this, I not only became more conscious of my own stress responses, but also shared my realisation openly with my team. I told them that if ever I seemed cold or withdrawn, it wasn't because I was annoyed or upset with anyone – it was simply a sign that I was completely absorbed in solving a problem. We even agreed on a little 'stop phrase' – or rather, a stop question: *Maria, are you saving the world right now, or do you have time for a chat?* This small ritual didn't just defuse potential tension; it also gave us a few light-hearted moments along the way.

Emotional predictability isn't about rigid self-control or striving for perfection. It's about understanding your own reactions, making yourself easier to read, more approachable, and a safer presence for those around you. And sometimes, while you're still working on that awareness, you can help others by giving them clear signals on how to interact with you when you're being crabby. (And, by the way, this works both ways.)

If you become predictable and open – someone others don't see as a threat – it will make it much easier, for both you and them, to engage in deep and difficult conversations.

Let's take a closer look.

THE difficult conversation

The business world is full of frameworks on how to give so-called corrective or developmental feedback. Many of them are well structured and effective. Take the classic 'sandwich' technique – start with something positive, move on to the criticism, then end on a high note. Or the 'strengths-based' approach, where you link the feedback to a person's existing strengths, showing how they can use it to improve.

Logical as these methods may be, they don't address the most crucial challenge: how do you have this conversation without sounding like you're following a script? How do you give feedback in a way that strengthens, rather than damages, your relationship with your team members? And finally – how do you get through it without losing a million nerve cells in the process?

Let me walk you through a technique built on my own trial and error as a manager – a collection of key points that have helped me and my clients prepare for and navigate difficult conversations, not just at work, but in everyday life as well.

Preparation:
- Make sure you have enough information to ground the conversation. Can you rely on facts, specific examples or, if needed, observations from others? It's especially important to revisit any agreements you previously made with the person you're about to speak with – were they clear enough? Were they properly discussed and agreed upon? These will serve as key reference points during the conversation.
- Have a clear sense of purpose. Think about your intentions. What do you actually want from this conversation? What's the outcome you're hoping for? Difficult discussions don't always go as planned – stress and emotions can throw you off course. But if you keep your purpose in mind, it'll be much easier to steer things in the right direction. And remember, the focus should be on the future – not *'You messed everything up'*, but *'What can we do differently next time?'*
- Get into the right mindset. Before you start, check in with yourself – what are you bringing into this conversation emotionally? No matter how carefully you phrase things, if your tone, body language or energy convey frustration or irritation, the other person will pick up on it. Whatever you're feeling, try to enter the conversation with a calm and open attitude – it will make a productive discussion far more likely.
- An optional but highly recommended step: practise with a generative AI tool like ChatGPT. It can help you refine your wording, spot any unconscious biases and even structure the conversation – where to start, how to transition and what to prioritise.
- Choose the right moment. Don't spring the conversation on them

out of the blue with a casual *'Got a minute?'* in an attempt to make it feel more relaxed. More often than not, this just catches the other person off guard and makes the conversation feel even more uncomfortable. Instead, plan ahead – either schedule a separate time or let them know in advance that your upcoming one-to-one will focus on a specific topic. If emotions are running high – anger, frustration, disappointment, or stress after a tough client meeting – it's often best to wait until things have settled down. Otherwise, you're likely to face a defensive reaction rather than a productive discussion. The same applies to addressing unhelpful behaviours – it's far more effective to give feedback when the person is in a different state of mind, rather than catching them in the moment.

The conversation:

- Be upfront from the start – let them know this won't be the easiest conversation. Don't soften the lead-in with small talk about the weather, the weekend or unrelated work updates. If you do, the shift to the real topic will feel awkward and jarring.
- Acknowledge your own responsibility. Could you have influenced the situation but didn't? Did you overlook the challenges they were facing? Have you put this conversation off for too long? Starting this way signals that this is a discussion between two human beings, not a kangaroo court – and it might just make them more open to what you have to say.
- Frame your message as a request for help – a chance to work together on finding a solution. *Could you help me understand what happened?* or *Could you help figure out how we should approach this?* This way, it becomes a conversation – something you both have a say in – rather than something being done *to* them.
- Choose your words carefully – language matters more than you might think. Focus on the task or the work itself, not the person.

If you criticise *them*, they'll instinctively become defensive. But if you point to something specific in their work, they're far more likely to want to *fix* it. Swap *'You're not strategic enough'* for *'Your presentation would be stronger if the strategy and logic were clearer.'* Avoid corporate jargon and sweeping statements like *'always'*, *'never'* or *'everyone'*. These make it harder to have a real conversation about what actually happened.

- Ask questions. Resist the urge to simply lay out *your* version of events and treat it as the starting point for the discussion. If you genuinely want to understand their perspective, keep asking questions until you do. Choose open, non-judgemental questions. Instead of *'How could you do that?'* – which instantly puts them on the defensive – try *'What led to that decision?'*
- Really listen! Be honest – how often do you start jumping to conclusions within the first few sentences? How quickly do you begin filling in the gaps with your own assumptions or opinions? Stay present and *validate* what the other person is saying – this is what turns a conversation into a genuine exchange.
- If, despite your best efforts, the conversation triggers a strong reaction – tears, for example – it might be best to pause and come back to it later. But don't let discomfort push you into cancelling the conversation altogether or backing down just to smooth things over. Stick with it – just give it time until emotions have settled.

At the end and after the conversation:

- Before wrapping up, take a moment to check in with yourself – does the conversation still align with the intention you set when preparing for it? Have you stayed on track or has the focus drifted?
- Make sure you leave the conversation with something concrete – if not a full resolution, then at least a clear next step that both

of you understand. Beyond the practicalities, it's also worth acknowledging how you feel at the end of the conversation – lighter? relieved? still unsure? – and asking the other person how they feel as well. There's no need to push for an answer, but giving them the space to share can be valuable in itself.

- After the conversation, take some time to reflect. How did you feel during it? Did you manage to find the right words? What might you do differently next time? Try stepping into the other person's shoes – how do you think they felt? How might they have interpreted what you said? And finally, imagine watching the conversation as a neutral observer. How did the exchange come across? Seeing it from a distance can often reveal things you might not have noticed in the moment.

Most importantly, remember that this is an interaction between two human beings – real people, with good intentions at heart, who sometimes make mistakes or misunderstand each other. You are no different from the person sitting in front of you – you just have different roles within the organisation. Humans have a remarkable ability to communicate, find common ground and resolve even the most complex issues – that's what sets us apart as a species. And this, too, is a challenge you can work through together.

What if the feedback is about you?

More and more companies are introducing manager evaluations, often allowing team members to submit their feedback anonymously if at least three people take part. If your company follows this system, the best approach, in my view, is to discuss the results openly with your team. Many managers keep these results to themselves, analysing them in private – often out of a sense of vulnerability or because they only want to take on board the parts they're ready to hear. However, even if your evaluation is filled with glowing reviews, it's worth taking a step back and discussing the feedback with your team. A positive score might reflect genuine appreciation, but it could also signal something else – perhaps people are reluctant to voice criticism, or they see the survey as just another corporate formality.

Let's look at the reverse situation – your team's feedback about you is negative. Your decisions are criticised and the way you work is causing frustration. Having an open conversation in this case takes real courage, but it's the only way to show your team that their opinions genuinely matter to you and that you're willing to meet them halfway. You don't have to agree with everything that's been said, but at the same time, don't let your natural defensive reactions – or the fear of losing face – get in the way.

To help with this, I encourage my clients to use a technique called Second Score, developed by Harvard Law School professor Sheila Heen. When you receive critical feedback, ask yourself: what score would I give myself for how I handled it? Say your performance rating was three out of ten. But when you reflect on how you took that feedback on board – whether you accepted it constructively, looked ahead and took steps to improve – you might rate yourself an eight out of ten. The value of this exercise can't be overstated. It shifts your focus inwards, helps you develop self-awareness and humility, and keeps you looking ahead – rather than getting caught up in defensiveness, self-doubt or resentment.

My friend Brian is a master of this technique, thanks to a story that shaped the way he approaches feedback. When he first stepped into a management role, he threw himself into it with boundless enthusiasm. He had a team of four and did everything he could to be a good leader. When delegating tasks, he took great care to explain exactly what needed to be done, corrected mistakes himself – sometimes even redoing reports – and shielded his team from criticism, always standing up for them with senior management. So, when the results of his first manager evaluation came in at the end of the year, he was stunned. The scores were low. He had expected the exact opposite – surely the team would appreciate how much he had done for them and leave nothing but fantastic feedback?

Despite feeling upset and confused, Brian chose to approach the situation the way he always did – with honesty, openness and a genuine desire to understand. So, he decided to meet with his team, lay his cards on the table, and have a frank discussion about how they worked together, his approach, and what could be done differently. The meeting turned out to be nothing like he expected. All four members of his team told him they appreciated his efforts, but working with him often made them feel like small children being fussed over by an overprotective father. They wanted to be independent, to voice their opinions, to experiment and even make mistakes – rather than feeling like someone was constantly stepping in to tidy up after them and making decisions on their behalf. They wanted to be treated as adults, as capable professionals, not infantilised under the watchful eye of a protective parent. For Brian, this was a real wake-up call. His determination to be a good manager had turned into overprotection, stifling his team's growth and preventing them from taking ownership. Instead of helping them become stronger, he realised he had unknowingly been holding them back from stepping up and proving themselves.

This story has a happy ending. After that first truly open conversation with his team, Brian reconsidered many aspects of his approach – including how often they would discuss their ways of working together. But if he hadn't had the courage to face the feedback with an open mind, he would have carried on believing he was doing everything right – while his team simply failed to appreciate it.

Feedback is a gift – but one you shouldn't wait to be given. Even if your company doesn't have a formal system for evaluating managers, it's important to hear from your team. Here's something to try: instead of asking for feedback directly, ask for their thoughts or advice on what you could do differently in the future. The word *feedback* naturally makes people look backwards, which is why you might hear something like, 'Everything was great, you're doing fine!' – nice to hear, but not particularly helpful for your development as a manager. By shifting the focus to the future, you open the door to more meaningful insights.

The way you respond to feedback will, to a great extent, shape how your team approaches both giving and receiving it. As I mentioned earlier, a manager is always a significant figure – whether you realise it or not, your team is constantly observing you and taking cues from your behaviour.

If you demonstrate that you're open to growth and change, acknowledge your mistakes, and model a mindset of humility and curiosity, your team is likely to do the same. And when that happens, feedback stops being a difficult conversation and turns into a genuine exchange – one that enriches both sides.

MISSION 3:

Make growth your survival strategy

In nature, a life system that doesn't adapt to the environment eventually disappears. The same thing happens in business – teams that don't learn to change eventually hit limits they can't overcome. The reality is that growth, development and adaptation aren't luxuries. They're survival strategies: if you don't evolve, you stagnate. And if you stagnate, you'll become irrelevant and wither away as the world passes you by.

Every manager – new or experienced – knows they should develop their team. But all too often, this idea is just a mantra with no real thought behind it – no personal perspective, no clear purpose, no real plan. *Why*, exactly, should the team be growing? *How* should they develop? Not everyone has a clear answer to these questions.

Some managers I know even talk about developing their people as if it were an act of heroism – an extra effort they're making on top of their regular work, which is supervising and evaluating the team's work. They add learning and development as a favour, a bonus they're generously giving their team, without realising something crucial:

You're not here to supervise or evaluate – you're here to make your team better. Every day.

If the people around you aren't developing, it's not just their problem – you personally won't get any further up the organisation: you're as high as you'll ever get. Your team's evolution stalls when growth isn't a priority. Your job as a manager is to help your people grasp this vital need, support their growth – and keep growing yourself.

Let's be practical: when people develop, take ownership and understand the meaning behind their work, they don't need endless instructions and handholding.

I've seen so many new managers fall into the same trap – especially when they've been promoted within their own team. It's one of the hardest transitions, psychologically: you have to redefine your relationships with former peers without damaging them, while also proving the value you bring in your new role. But what does that value actually look like?

Many default to what they know best: doing the same work they did before – but for the whole team. After all, they know how to do it 'right', don't they? As a result, instead of helping the team grow, they multiply their own workload. At some point, the manager turns into a multi-armed Shiva – until they burn out completely.

And what's left? A burnt-out manager and a team that hasn't grown. *In the end, a leader's worth isn't measured by how much they take on, but by how much they elevate the people around them.*

Another mistake I often see new managers make is grabbing onto a ready-made set of 'proven practices' as if they're a lifeline. They arm themselves with frameworks, playbooks and HR-approved development plans and send their teams to training sessions, believing that's what growth looks like. And that's where the 'cargo cult' kicks in – following the rituals, ticking all the right boxes but never truly taking responsibility for their team's development.

But while you're busy going through the motions of developing your team, the world isn't standing still. We've seen not just individuals but entire companies – like Kodak and Nokia – fall behind because they stayed in their comfort zone. The same applies to managers: if you rely only on what works today, you might wake up tomorrow and realise the world has moved on without you.

One of the biggest shifts right now is AI. Many managers are understandably concerned – not just about their own roles, but about their teams. Will their expertise still be needed? Will their skills remain relevant? The concern is valid, but the response shouldn't be panic. It should be growth.

Not growth to outrun AI – that's not realistic. But growth that helps you shift your value – from doing the work to deciding what's worth doing. From execution to judgement, creativity and meaningful connection.

That's why both your own learning and your team's should focus not just on 'keeping up', but on staying relevant: learning to make better decisions, take on more complex problems, and work with AI as a partner – not a rival. We'll explore these skills in more depth in Mission 5, where we look at systems thinking, strategy and navigating internal dynamics. But for now, the key is to see development not as a bonus, but as a way to future-proof your team – and yourself.

I don't think AI will replace everyone. But it will absolutely replace those who operate on cargo cult thinking – forwarding messages from leadership, distributing checklists and calling that 'development'.

Which brings us to a simple truth:

Growing your team isn't just for their benefit. It's for yours, too.

Developing your team isn't just a nice-to-have. It's a necessity. So the question is: how do you make it work? Even the best intentions can lead nowhere if you're ignoring two critical factors:

1. What's holding people back? (Because no amount of motivation helps if someone keeps hitting the same walls.)
2. What's driving them forward? (Because growth isn't about forcing people – it's about tapping into what truly moves them.)

Removing the barriers to growth

A friend of mine, Emma, who's also a coach, once shared a metaphor that stayed with me. She said she sees her role as clearing a riverbed – removing the blockages that slow the current so the water can regain its flow and become clearer and stronger as it moves. It struck me as a perfect way to think about growth.

You can't *force* water to move in a certain direction. But you *can* remove what's in its way.

The same applies to people. You can't *make* someone more curious, driven or open to change. But you *can* help them recognise what's holding them back – and clear the path so they can move forward.

There's another layer to it. Psychologist Edward de Bono introduced the concept of 'rivers of thinking' – the idea that our habits and assumptions carve deep mental grooves, much like rivers shaping landscapes over time. The longer we follow the same patterns, the harder it becomes to step outside them. That's why it's not just about removing obstacles – it's also about helping the water find new, unexpected directions. The same goes for people: sometimes, they don't need a push, just a shift in perspective – so instead of following the same well-worn path, they start to see possibilities they hadn't even considered.

MAKE PEOPLE THINK

With the rise of generative AI and the spread of cargo cult thinking, it's never been easier to switch off your brain and reach for quick, packaged solutions. But that's the last thing you want for your team.

The brain is like a muscle – it needs regular training and the right fuel to grow stronger. And in a world that's constantly shifting, the real skill isn't just learning, but *relearning* – staying open to new ideas, seeing things from different angles, knowing when to explore new paths and when to abandon failing strategies.

So yes, you and your team need learning. But not just any

learning. Not all training is useful and not all information leads to growth. What matters is choosing the right kind – deliberate, well thought out and relevant.

What's in your arsenal?

Training and courses are the first things that come to mind. Whether it's in-house sessions, external programmes, business-school courses or professional training, it's not just about offering learning opportunities for the sake of it – it's about helping people choose the ones that will actually make a difference in their work.

So, what's worth investing time in? Something that helps them see things from a fresh perspective – *thinking beyond the usual limits*. For example: a product manager taking a psychology course to understand customer behaviour better. Or something that helps them fill in their gaps or blind spots – the skills they're missing that could take them to the next level. For example: a brilliant analyst struggling to present to clients taking a course in public speaking for introverts.

If your company doesn't pay for training – which is often the case – you can't push employees to invest in it themselves. That should always be their choice. Luckily, there are plenty of free (or nearly free) courses on platforms like Coursera or Khan Academy, so learning is always an option.

And don't be afraid to get creative! You can design and run a workshop yourself – giving both you and your team fresh perspectives while having a great time together. Here are just a few ideas to spark your imagination:

- Pixar Storytelling Rules in Action – host a session where your team generates business ideas or solutions using Pixar's famous twenty-two storytelling principles. For example, try framing new consumer offers using the classic Pixar script template:

'Once upon a time, there was ___. Every day, ___. One day, ___. Because of that, ___. Because of that, ___. Until finally ___.'

> Here's an example: 'Once upon a time, people everywhere struggled to keep their socks paired. Every day, they would rummage through drawers, frustrated by mysterious sock disappearances. One day, we designed the 'Sock Mate 3000' – a revolutionary gadget that tracks your socks in real time. Because of that, mismatched pairs became a thing of the past. Because of that, laundry day turned from a headache into a triumph. Until finally, no one had to face the shame of wearing one blue sock and one polka-dotted sock ever again.'

- Lego Strategy Workshop – bring out a box of LEGO bricks and use them to model business processes, brainstorm creative solutions or explore team dynamics in a hands-on way. For example, ask your team to build a step-by-step representation of a customer's experience with your product or service and tell the story which brings to life what they've built. This visual approach can uncover hidden pain points and inspire fresh ideas for improvement.
- The Anti-Conference – a day where each team member shares their biggest failures and worst decisions, followed by a discussion on what lessons can be learned from them.
- Role-Play Pitch Challenge – turn your meeting room into a stage! Assign roles – clients, external partners, competitors and internal team members – and act out real-life business scenarios. See what happens when your team has to think on their feet, defend their ideas and adapt their strategy in real time.

Given that I'm writing this book, it'd be a bit strange not to talk about books, wouldn't it? There's a wealth of knowledge available – not only books but lectures, articles and open content from experts in your field. However, while this kind of learning is valuable for sparking curiosity and broadening perspectives, it shouldn't be aimless.

We all know people who proudly claim to read a business book a week. But the truth is, many people read business books the way they read fiction – as a story about someone else's experiences.

One colleague of mine was particularly memorable for the impressive library he built next to his desk – stacked with biographies and memoirs of legendary business leaders and athletes. But when I once asked him whether he applied any of their advice, he simply shrugged and said, *'I just find their stories inspiring – these people are on a whole different level!'*

And that's exactly why it's so important not just to absorb knowledge but actually *think it through and find ways to use it in real life.*

If someone on your team tells you they enjoyed a book or an article, don't just nod – ask them: *'What stood out to you? Why? What have you found effective to use?'* See if they're connecting what they read to how they think or act moving forward.

We live in a world of short-form content, where quick insights are everywhere. That's why articles and publications from industry experts or respected media can be a great way to stay up to date. (And yes, I realise the irony of saying this in a book – but don't worry, I've kept it much shorter than Leo Tolstoy's *War and Peace*.) That said, don't just stick to industry-specific content – broaden your view. Read *The Wall Street Journal*, *The Financial Times* or insight papers from McKinsey and BCG. The more perspectives you take in, the better you'll understand how the world really works. It's not just about staying informed – it sharpens your judgement and helps you spot cause-and-effect patterns faster.

Why is it important not just to read books and online resources with your team but to actually discuss them? Because it's not just about learning new things – it's about building a shared understanding.

When your team shares similar perspectives and values, it doesn't just improve workflows – it shifts the entire team dynamic. You develop a common language and way of thinking, which means decisions come faster, there's less time wasted on explanations and alignment happens more naturally. You create an environment where there's no need to keep justifying *why* something matters – because everyone already gets it.

But more than that, it creates a real sense of belonging and engagement. Talking about ideas – whether through books, articles or even films – doesn't just sharpen skills, it brings people closer. It turns colleagues into a team, not just working side by side but sharing something bigger: a common way of thinking, a shared perspective on what matters and a sense of purpose in what they do.

Where else can people gain new knowledge and insights? At work! Give your team opportunities to step outside their usual tasks – whether it's collaborating on cross-functional projects, working with other departments or simply spending time in a different role. Learning from colleagues is just as valuable as formal training. Set up 'shadowing' opportunities, where they can sit in on key meetings, observe negotiations or watch experienced professionals in action. Sometimes, the best lessons don't come from a textbook – they come from seeing how things really get done.

Help people see what's holding them back

Lately, coaching has been treated as the ultimate tool for growth and the go-to remedy for poor performance. Something's not working? Coach them. Need to develop your team? Coach them.

Coaching doesn't replace learning.

You can't coach someone into knowledge they simply don't have. And yet, I keep seeing managers try – asking a junior hire who started a month ago, 'What do you think the best solution is?' or 'What advice would you give someone in your situation?' No wonder they stare back in confusion.

Coaching is a powerful tool – but only when used at the right time and in the right context. Before jumping into it, ask yourself: *does my team have the skills and knowledge they need to grow?* If not, that's your first step. Because while some barriers come from within, others are simply down to a lack of tools to work with.

Coaching helps people identify the fears, limiting beliefs and blind spots that hold them back. It's about exploration, not delivering a single correct answer or a quick fix. Real change happens as a natural consequence of this process – when people gain new insights, spot patterns they hadn't noticed before and see the bigger picture in a different way. Abraham Maslow put it beautifully: *'What is necessary to change a person is to change his awareness of himself.'*

If we simplify it, the coaching process can be broken down into three key steps:

Step 1 – Explore the current situation
How does the person see their situation? What facts, emotions and perspectives are involved? What's missing – what do we not yet know?

Step 2 – Understand what's behind it
What beliefs, emotions or habits are at play? How can we look at this from a broader perspective? What has the person not noticed before?

Step 3 – Explore possible paths and resources
What could help in this situation? What new opportunities are emerging? How can this awareness be applied?

Of course, coaching isn't about following a rigid structure – it's about having a meaningful conversation that helps the other person uncover insights and new possibilities. But like any skill, good coaching requires practice, and I strongly recommend getting at least some form of training rather than trying to rely on intuition alone. Even a short course can make a big difference in understanding what coaching really is (and what it isn't), how to ask better questions and how to avoid the common traps managers fall into when they start using coaching with their teams. These traps could be, for example, falling into therapy conversations by discussing childhood traumas, or by trying to provide them with the 'right answers'.

Resist the temptation to jump to conclusions, make assumptions or share how you once solved a similar problem – no matter how hard it is to hold back. I still remember how baffled I was during my first corporate coaching session. My coach, a senior manager from another region, barely let me get two minutes into my story before cutting me off: 'Oh, I get it! This reminds me of something from my own experience with xyz. And you know what I realised back then . . . ?' What followed was a long-winded story about himself – one that, unsurprisingly and disappointingly, had nothing to do with my situation.

One of the great strengths of successful managers is their ability to find quick and effective solutions. But in a coaching conversation, you need to set that aside. Your role here isn't to jump in with advice – it's to ask open questions, seek clarity and listen without judgement. Unlike mentoring, where one person takes on the role of teacher or guide, coaching is a conversation between equals. When a manager acts as a coach, their position in the hierarchy – and the symbolic psychological power we discussed in the previous chapter – can make it harder for the coachee to open up fully. They might hold back, filter what they say or hesitate to express their real thoughts and feelings.

That's why trust is everything. If someone trusts you enough to open up, never abuse that trust and use it against them. You need to be ready for the fact that coaching may lead your team members to insights that don't align with your own interests. They might realise they want to switch departments, move to another company or even leave the country. Let them. Don't try to hold them back, manipulate them or make them feel guilty.

I learned this lesson the hard way. After a series of development conversations with my manager, I had a realisation – I wanted to gain experience working in another market. Up until then, my entire career had been in one country. I had always worked with international clients and teams, but I'd never worked abroad myself. The idea felt inspiring, energising – so I shared it with my manager, thinking he'd be supportive.

His reaction caught me off guard. *'You're leaving?'* he asked, his tone somewhere between disbelief and disappointment. I explained that it was just a thought – I hadn't even started planning anything yet. I just wanted to share what I'd realised through our conversations and how grateful I was for them.

I walked away thinking nothing had changed. But I was wrong. Almost immediately, I noticed the shift – he kept his distance, excluded me from discussions, handed key projects to others. And then, a few weeks later, a colleague pulled me aside and said, *'Just so you know, he thinks you turned your back on the team.'*

That was a turning point for me. I understood how easy it is for managers to feel possessive of their teams, even without realising it. It's human nature – when you invest in someone's growth, a part of you hopes they'll stay. But helping people grow means being ready for the moment they might outgrow their current role – and sometimes, even your team.

Since then, I've seen many of my former team members move into new roles, take on bigger challenges and even become managers themselves. And I've made a conscious effort to support them rather than hold them back.

Hard as it might be to acknowledge it, your team members are not your assets. You work with them – you don't own them.

So be decent. Be generous. Let them grow (or even go). And you'll grow, too.

Helping people grow

Helping people grow isn't just about offering support – it's also about setting expectations. Managers often face a delicate challenge: how do you set a high bar for your team – both in strategy and in daily work – while also keeping them motivated and making sure their efforts are recognised? At first glance, these two ideas might seem to pull in opposite directions.

If you focus too much on high expectations, it's easy to become overly critical, always noticing what's lacking and, in the process, draining people's motivation. On the other hand, if you always focus on the positive and only offer praise and encouragement, you risk turning into a caretaker rather than a leader – someone who keeps people comfortable but doesn't push them to grow. In the end, both the team's development and its results suffer.

David Yeager, a psychologist and professor at the University of Texas, is one of the leading researchers on the *Growth Mindset*. He developed a model originally designed to help teenagers and young adults (aged ten to twenty-five) build resilience and motivation, but it works just as well in a manager–team dynamic. At its heart is the idea that high expectations and strong support don't contradict each other – they go hand in hand.

Rather than simply criticising or encouraging people, a manager applies the *High Standards & High Support* approach:

> 'I am setting a high standard for you, because I know you are capable of meeting it. I will make sure you have everything you need to get there – guidance, resources and support.'

This does two things at once. It shows that you take the person seriously, that you trust their abilities. But it also challenges them – it makes clear that they have something to strive for.

And here's the crucial part: even if you, as a manager, create the right conditions for growth, provide tools and resources to build skills, coaching and support, the choice to step up still belongs to the individual. Motivation needs to come from within.

'I believe in you, but it's up to you to take the leap.'

A manager can only do half the job – setting the stage, offering resources and creating an environment where people can develop. The other half? That's down to them.

But what does this actually look like in practice? Let's take a real example.

High Standards & High Support in Action

Alan was at his breaking point. Michael, one of his team members, was *brilliant* – constantly reading, attending conferences, keeping up with every social media trend. But when it came to client proposals, he was a disaster. Every presentation was over a hundred slides, packed with every possible detail. No structure. No clear narrative. Just a stream of consciousness.

'I don't understand,' Alan sighed. *'Michael's one of the smartest people I know. But every time I ask for a simple, clear pitch, I get... this.'* And so, Alan would step in – rewriting slides, cutting unnecessary content, doing the work himself.

At first, it felt like he was helping. But over time, nothing changed. Michael's decks stayed chaotic and Alan was stuck playing editor-in-chief. It was a classic trap: Alan thought he was being supportive, but in reality, he was creating dependency.

Something had to change. With his own coach, Alan broke the problem down into three layers – and tackled each one differently.

1. The daily work: client presentations
Instead of reworking Michael's slides himself, Alan set clear expectations:

'Next time, you should do no more than twenty slides. Three key takeaways. Each slide should focus on one message, with a clear flow.'

He sat down with Michael to discuss what makes a strong presentation, went through standout examples and discussed the structure behind them. He also stopped micromanaging edits and instead asked Michael to present his drafts and explain his choices – forcing him to justify his decisions and think critically.

High standards: Alan expected clear, concise and strategic presentations.

High support: he provided examples, guidance and space to improve.

2. The skill gap: structuring and prioritisation
Michael wasn't deliberately making bad presentation decks – he just lacked the skill to prioritise and structure. His instinct was to include everything, thinking more information meant better decisions.

Alan gave him tools to improve. He suggested books like *The Pyramid Principle* by Barbara Minto, online courses on strategic thinking and small assignments where Michael had to summarise complex topics in just five slides.

High standards: Alan expected Michael to learn how to structure information.

High support: he provided resources, training and hands-on practice.

3. The deeper issue: mindset and anxiety
But there was something deeper at play. Through coaching, Alan uncovered the real issue: Michael was afraid.

For Michael, knowledge felt like a safety net – his defence against mistakes, criticism and uncertainty. He believed that missing even one detail could expose him as less of an expert – and eventually, cost him his job.

Alan helped Michael see that expertise isn't about knowing everything – it's about distilling what matters and communicating it well.

Together, they worked on breaking the pattern: setting time limits for research; unsubscribing from some of the overwhelming content sources; encouraging Michael to speak at conferences, not just listen.

Michael's biggest realisation? Drowning in information wasn't making him an expert – it was stopping him from becoming one.

High standards: Alan helped Michael redefine expertise and confidence.

High support: he coached him through the anxiety and helped shift his mindset.

Alan had done his part – he had set the bar high, provided the right support and helped Michael step out of the pattern that was holding him back. But ultimately, it was Michael who had to take the leap. And that's the crucial point: you can create the conditions for growth, but real change only happens when people want it for themselves.

Motivation and incentives for growth

We've already looked at what holds people back – barriers that slow or even block growth. But even when those obstacles are removed, there remains a second, crucial question: what drives people forward? Growth isn't something you can simply impose; it blossoms when someone feels genuinely motivated to progress. And that's precisely where many managers find themselves at an impasse: how can you create an environment in which growth is not only possible but actively desired?

I often hear managers say, *'My people are only interested in growth if it comes with a promotion and a pay rise.'*

At first glance, that seems perfectly reasonable – who wouldn't want more money and a step up the career ladder? Yet this assumption often mirrors corporate norms rather than reflecting individual aspirations. In many organisations, career growth is viewed almost exclusively in terms of salary increases and job titles. While companies may tout personal development, learning and impact, in practice the only rewards that truly matter are financial.

This narrow perspective distorts motivation. Of course, salary is important – it would be naive to say otherwise – but true engagement isn't built on pay alone. Recognition, alignment with company goals, the thrill of shared achievements and a sense of higher purpose all play their part. Still, because promotions are so frequently upheld as the ultimate reward, managers can feel utterly powerless when they're unable to offer one.

The issue runs deeper. Many corporate cultures treat promotions as a carrot to be dangled, structuring entire systems around grade progression. In environments where climbing the ladder is the sole measure of success – or where an 'up or out' mentality prevails – those who don't aspire to senior leadership are often unfairly viewed as lacking ambition. I've seen highly skilled professionals, who chose to deepen their expertise rather than manage others, labelled as 'not driven enough'. In annual reviews, they were urged to develop leadership skills as if their current path were somehow incomplete. I find that a rather narrow, limiting perspective.

The reality is that not everyone wants – or is suited – to a senior leadership role and that's perfectly fine. Yet many new managers struggle to accept this because they project their own ambitions onto their teams. They reached where they are by actively pursuing that path, so the idea that someone might choose a different route feels foreign. But ambition comes in many forms. Choosing to master a craft rather than move into management isn't a lack of ambition – it's simply a different way to grow.

REFRAMING THE CONVERSATION

When employees say they expect a promotion, they're often expressing something deeper: *'I want to feel valued. I want my contribution to be recognised. I want new challenges.'*

The key is to broaden their perspective and show that growth isn't a binary choice between promotion and stagnation. There are many ways to feel challenged, valued and impactful – several of which lie within your control as a manager.

That's why, when someone says, *'I'm doing my job well, am I getting promoted?'*, the best response isn't just a yes-or-no answer but an open conversation that helps them reframe their expectations:

- Doing your job well is the baseline. It's what's expected by default. Real growth comes from stepping beyond your defined role.
- Work is a game of limited resources. Not everyone can be promoted. The best way to compete for opportunities is to develop, contribute more and increase your visibility.
- Promotion isn't the only way to grow. There are other levers for progress – ones that you, as a manager, can help pull.

To illustrate this, let's look at three key drivers that can shift the focus from promotion to more sustainable sources of motivation. (Of course, there are other factors – such as a sense of higher purpose, personal mastery or creative autonomy – but these examples provide a practical starting point.)

1. Recognition

People don't always talk about it, yet recognition is one of the most powerful motivators. We all need to see our value reflected back to us. At work, a manager is the most important mirror of an employee's worth, but recognition isn't limited to your direct feedback – it also comes from senior leadership, colleagues, clients and even the wider industry.

Recognition can take many forms: visibility in front of top management, public praise from colleagues and clients, inclusion in a talent programme, invitations to high-profile projects, award nominations and more.

How to frame the conversation:

'I can't guarantee you a promotion, but I can promise you this: if we initiate something that hasn't been done before, I will make sure your impact is recognised at the highest level. Great work benefits the business – and visibility benefits you. And that, in turn, can open doors to future opportunities.'

2. Linking individual work to company priorities

According to a McKinsey study,[1] this factor is just as important for employee performance as differentiated pay and coaching from a manager. People feel more motivated when they can clearly see how their work contributes to the company's priorities. This isn't just about ticking tasks off the list – it's about seeing the real impact of what you do and knowing that your efforts count.

On the flip side, when people lose sight of how their efforts connect to company priorities, their motivation inevitably drops. At some point, work starts to feel like a series of disconnected tasks rather than part of something bigger.

How to frame the conversation (for example, with a data analyst):

'I can't guarantee you a promotion, but I want to show you how the insights you generate directly shape high-level business decisions. Your work isn't just about numbers – it's solving a crucial problem for our company. The more you refine your expertise, the more valuable your contributions become.'

---

[1] https://www.mckinsey.com/capabilities/people-and-organizational-performance/our-insights/straight-talk-about-employee-evaluation-and-performance-management

3. Team Achievements

Beyond individual recognition, people are also motivated by a sense of belonging and pride in shared success. It's not merely about working together; it's also about healthy competition. When teams compete and achieve together, it fuels ambition, pushes individuals to stretch their limits and creates a natural drive to excel.

How to frame the conversation:

> *'I can't guarantee you a promotion, but I want you to see how our team's success boosts our influence within the company. The better we perform, the more resources, responsibilities and opportunities we gain – and that strengthens your personal positioning for future growth.'*

These aren't rigid scripts but rather conversation starters designed to expand the scope of motivation beyond simple transactional thinking. The aim is to shift the focus from the transactional 'good work = automatic promotion' to a longer-term view of value and influence.

BEYOND PROMOTION: REINVENTING THE ROLE

When people talk about promotion, it isn't always about career ambition – it can be about escaping a role that no longer excites them. When the day-to-day becomes repetitive or uninspiring, the natural assumption is that growth must come from moving up or moving on.

But another way to reignite motivation is to reinvent the role itself. Instead of seeing a job as something fixed, it helps to apply a *growth mindset* – not just to the person, but to their responsibilities. What you need to do is to break down the role into its key elements and explore which aspects can be expanded, developed or taken on more actively – aligned with what drives them – while handing over certain tasks to others where possible (perhaps even to AI eventually). This approach allows people to shape their work in a way that makes it more meaningful, even when no immediate career moves are on the horizon.

Growth needs a roadmap

To ensure that a team member's growth isn't just a vague aspiration but a structured, shared plan, it helps to map out how everyday actions contribute to longer-term goals. A simple framework can provide much-needed clarity:

Categories	Immediate Priorities (0.5–1 year)	Future Ambitions (2–5 years)
What do I want to achieve? *(Your vision for this timeframe)*		
Hard skills to develop *(Specific knowledge or tools to master)*		
Soft skills to develop *(Behavioural or emotional intelligence areas)*		
Beyond-role opportunities *(Projects or initiatives to serve the priority)*		

Not everyone will have a clear answer straight away about what they want to achieve. Some simply haven't thought about their development in structured terms before. Others may default to the most obvious next step – *'I want to become a senior specialist'* or *'I'd like to lead a team'* –

without considering what truly excites them. As a manager, helping people articulate what they genuinely want from their careers can be transformative. It's not just about motivation; it's about expanding their sense of possibility.

This framework is valuable even when someone ultimately wants to transition into a different function. It ensures you both stay aligned on the necessary steps, making the process both intentional and structured.

I once worked with a sales manager who gradually realised that his real passion lay in marketing. It wasn't a sudden revelation but something that became clearer through our coaching conversations – and, eventually, through the structured career planning we did together. I won't pretend it was easy for me to accept, as he was exceptional at sales, but my personal feelings weren't a reason to stand in his way.

Instead of forcing an immediate leap, we used the framework to map out a plan that allowed him to explore and test this new direction while continuing to grow in his current role. Over the course of nine months, he:

- took on cross-functional projects with the marketing team
- enrolled in relevant training
- arranged shadowing opportunities with a senior marketing leader.

By doing this, he not only gained experience but also built relationships, proved his value and ensured this was genuinely the right move. Meanwhile, I started preparing for his replacement and our sales team benefited from having an *ambassador* inside another key function. When the transition finally happened nine months later, it was structured, planned and beneficial for everyone involved. As is often the case with talented people, he didn't just step into marketing – he made an impact from day one, becoming a natural bridge between our two departments.

Your team's strongest growth driver?

As we wrap up this chapter on growth and development, there's one factor we simply cannot overlook – perhaps the most powerful motivator of all.

You.

Many of the most accomplished people I know, looking back on their careers, say something like: *'I remember my favourite manager – because she was the reason I started to grow. She was the one who truly inspired me!'*

Why does this matter? Firstly, because to support, coach and develop others effectively, you need to have *credibility*. If you're not continually learning, if you don't acknowledge your mistakes, if you don't demonstrate genuine humility, why would your team trust you to guide them? They won't be open about their blind spots or aspirations with a leader who appears to have none of their own.

Secondly, whether you realise it or not, your team is always watching. They calibrate themselves against you. That's why you must set a high bar – not only for them but for yourself. When your team sees you pitching bold ideas to leadership, challenging the status quo, writing for respected publications, enrolling in courses on AI or speaking at major conferences, they see more than just a manager. They see someone to aspire to, someone they're proud to work with.

And this influence often proves more powerful than direct management efforts. When you grow, your team grows – not out of obligation but with genuine intention. That's what transforms development from a strategy for surviving into one for *thriving*.

Who was the leader who truly inspired you to grow?
What will your team say about you?

MISSION 4:

Turn your team into your biggest project

How often do we blame external circumstances, other people or sheer bad luck for failing to accomplish our goals in life? In those moments, it feels like things are happening *to* us, leaving us with no choice but to react. Our mind naturally looks for a way to protect us: it shifts the blame to external factors so we don't have to face the discomfort of feeling powerless. But the truth is, much of what happens is shaped by our own choices – whether we want to acknowledge it or not.

For a new manager, figuring out how to build a strong team can be the hardest part of the job. It's the first real proof of leadership – and a direct challenge to one's capabilities. Managing only your own work is no longer enough – it's not about individual performance any more. Now, you're responsible for something bigger than yourself – a team that needs to be strong, not just functional. From now on it's about what you can build *together*.

Does it make sense to take a step back, get your bearings and figure things out when you start? Of course. But for some, it's much easier to latch onto a ready-made explanation for why the team isn't working the way you want.

I often hear new managers say, *'This is just the team I've been given.'* Many new managers see their team as something set in stone, something they just have to work with. Blaming the way things are feels comforting, almost reasonable.

When I hear someone shifting responsibility onto their boss, their partners or their team, I ask a single question: *'How does this situation serve you?'*

Early in my management career, I saw first-hand how avoiding responsibility leads you down a *cul-de-sac*. Alexander joined our agency and inherited a team of two from his predecessor – both were inexperienced and somewhat lost. Six months in, results weren't great, and Alexander constantly blamed this on the situation: the client was difficult, there weren't enough resources, and his team was too junior and weak. According to him, they'd need another five years to become competent, yet there wasn't enough justification to fire them either. Maybe the leadership got tired of Alexander's complaints or maybe they genuinely believed his reasoning, but they gave him an extra person. Strangely enough, the new hire turned out to be just like him – constantly blaming circumstances and making excuses for poor results. Instead of working, they spent their time moaning: *'This client has no idea what they want'; 'They keep demanding the impossible'; 'We just got the worst possible client'.*

Another six months passed, and their client terminated the contract with our agency. Alexander, the 'helpless victim of circumstances' was let go. I'm sure he still sees it as grossly unfair and nothing more than a cruel twist of fate.

Alexander's mistake is common. But the real danger isn't just blaming circumstances – it's what happens next. *The moment you decide nothing can change, you give yourself permission to stay stuck.* Because if it's out of your hands, then you're off the hook, right? And maybe that's the real reason behind this mindset – staying where you are feels safer than stepping up to the challenge. If you stop hiding behind excuses and start making real choices, you might surprise yourself with what you and your team are actually capable of achieving.

Let's test your thinking for a moment. Here's a question for you:

If you had a magic wand and could change one thing about your team, what would it be?

Your answer reveals what you currently see as fixed, as something that *just is*.

Now, a follow-up question: *Do you really need a magic wand for this? What could you change now – at least in part?*

You have far more influence than you might think. Believing this shifts your mindset from *'I'm just doing what I can within the given conditions'* to recognising the full scale of what's possible and giving yourself agency in the issue.

Your team isn't a lottery ticket you were handed when you became a manager – random numbers that either line up or don't, no matter what you do. Your team is your most important project. Like any project, its success depends far less on the conditions you inherited and far more on the decisions you make and the strategy you choose.

And, like any project, it won't run itself. You can't just sit back and accept the status quo.

Here's why:

If you're not hiring strong people, you're settling for mediocrity. Deep down, you might be afraid of not being *'the smartest person in the room'*.

If you tolerate low performers and passengers, you're weakening the team and demotivating your top players.

If you're afraid to let someone go, it means you value comfort more than excellence.

Managers often say, *'I'm not happy with what I've been given as a team'*. But let's turn that question around:

- Would top performers be happy to be in your team?
- If you had a choice, would you want to work in your own team?

If the answer isn't positive, it's a sign change is needed. And that starts with who you bring in and who you let go.

How do you make those decisions? Let's talk about how to make hiring a deliberate choice – not a gamble.

Hire people who raise the bar for you and for others

Let's start with the most fundamental question in building a team: who?

For decades, advice on hiring has been the same: *Find the strongest. The smartest. The best of the best.* Conventional wisdom says: hire A-players – top-performing individuals who don't just deliver results – they set the standard, shape the direction and push the company forward. They are proactive, ambitious, highly skilled and fully accountable for the outcome.

Wow. Sounds impressive, doesn't it? With people like this, you could invent perpetual motion, cure ageing and travel to Mars – even build a colony there. Hiring 'A players' sounds logical, but there's a fatal flaw: hiring for raw talent doesn't build a great team. It builds a collection of high-achieving individuals, each running their own race.

While it's true that your objective is to build the team out of strong people, please bear in mind that not every 'best' person actually makes the team better. This is why it makes sense to rethink what 'strong' really means.

We're living in an era where AI is advancing fast, making hard and tech skills less and less of a unique advantage. Meanwhile, interpersonal skills are only becoming more valuable. That's why the A-players of the future aren't the 'divas' that former Google CEO Eric Schmidt famously advocated hiring, but empathetic leaders – people who don't just deliver results but elevate those around them.

In a world where the highest positions in business and politics are often taken by those with oversized egos, dominant alpha aggression, and, let's be honest, even psychopathic traits, kindness is still too often mistaken for weakness, dullness or a lack of edge. But that's simply not true.

People with high emotional intelligence and strong ethical principles are just as capable of driving breakthroughs – the problem is, history hasn't given them many chances. And yes, I am talking about women – or, to put it more accurately, about those who don't fit the traditional alpha-male mould. Shifting this balance is, in many ways, in the hands of a new generation of managers, and I hope you choose to move in this direction.

What does this actually mean for hiring? My advice is simple: prioritise interpersonal skills, ability to connect genuinely with others and personal potential – particularly a candidate's proactivity, accountability and ability to think beyond the obvious. Instead of just ticking off experience and technical skills, focus on how they approach problems and make decisions. So instead of asking, *Who is the strongest?* start asking, *Who makes the team stronger?*

That's especially relevant because, as a new manager, you're probably not in a position to hire the most recognised industry experts. But here's the good news: the best people aren't always the most senior, high-profile candidates with impressive CVs. In fact, many of these 'seasoned' professionals have spent years adapting to corporate life – either as relentless go-getters chasing success at any cost or as individuals who follow the rules without questioning them.

The strongest candidate isn't always the loudest, the most decorated or the most traditionally impressive. Instead, ask yourself: does this person elevate those around them? Do they make teamwork easier or harder? Would I trust them to develop others, not just themselves?

And most importantly: *would I want this person to lead my team one day?*

Even if that's not on your radar yet, think about it: your team isn't just about today – it's about the future. Any team member of yours can eventually become your successor. So every hire should be someone you'd be proud to pass the torch to: someone not only effective and result-oriented, but also motivated by shared achievement rather than personal glory.

A few years ago, I witnessed first-hand how the wrong choice of successor – someone high-performing but fundamentally ego-driven – can quietly dismantle even the strongest team.

I had worked with Ian for a while, and there was no doubt he was one of the top performers in his department. He was sharp, ambitious and always in the spotlight – his results spoke for themselves. His manager, while acknowledging his sometimes overbearing nature, tolerated it because Ian delivered. Meanwhile, the rest of the team, just as competent but far less vocal, remained in the background.

When his manager left the company, the choice seemed obvious to our senior leadership: Ian was the natural successor. He was visible, outspoken and had a track record of success. But what they didn't see – or rather, what they never thought to question – was what kind of people leader he would become.

From day one, Ian made it clear that things had changed. He distanced himself from his former peers, drawing a sharp line between himself and the team: he acted like he was doing them a favour by agreeing to be their manager. He took full credit for successes, made a show of personally fixing 'their' mistakes and subtly undermined anyone who challenged him. He wasn't leading – he was performing. And the more he positioned himself as the lone genius, the more the team felt isolated, unheard and demotivated.

Because the team was so capable, they still delivered. Sales numbers hit record highs. To senior management, this was proof that they'd made the right choice. And Ian, of course, basked in the recognition.

It took a couple of years for the cracks to show. One by one, the team members left – some moving on to better roles, others simply burning out. By the time Ian was finally pushed out, thanks to a brutal manager feedback survey, there wasn't much of the original team left. The department had to be rebuilt almost from scratch.

This isn't a cautionary tale about one bad leader. It's about a common mistake: hiring – or promoting – based on individual brilliance, without asking the most important question: what kind of leader will this person become? When exceptional talent is coupled with that kind of self-focus, it seldom shifts – even when training or years of experience come their way. Ian was an A-player, no doubt. But when the wrong kind of A-player is put in charge, they don't just fail as a leader – they take the whole team down with them.

Now that we've covered *who* to hire, let's talk about *how* to hire.

Hiring do's and don'ts

Hiring mistakes happen to everyone – not just new managers. Even at the highest levels, a poor hiring decision can be disastrous, sometimes bringing down an entire company with it. Hiring is always a risk. No one can guarantee that a new hire will live up to expectations or turn out to be a true star.

But that doesn't mean you shouldn't do everything in your power to bring the best possible player onto your team. That part is entirely up to you.

I've made my fair share of hiring mistakes, and I've seen the same happen to colleagues. Most mistakes come down to one thing: a manager's willingness to compromise when building their team. The moment you accept that a compromise *might* be necessary – for whatever reason – you start a chain reaction. At first, the impact seems small. But in the long run, it can cost you more than you realise.

'He's not exactly what we were looking for, but we need to fill the role quickly.'

'She's not perfect, but it's hard to find someone better.'

'This candidate isn't a star, but at least they'll fill the gap – we just need extra hands.'

The minute you settle, you're setting yourself up for future problems – lower standards, frustration in the team, weaker results. Sooner or later, you'll have to either start over or accept mediocrity. And that's the real danger – because after a while, you stop even noticing it.

The most common hiring mistakes I've seen (and made myself):

Mistake 1: Not knowing exactly who you need – or why

This doesn't just slow down the hiring process and massively increase the risk of bringing in the wrong person. It also makes life harder for the candidate, for you, and for the entire team once they're on board. In short, it's the jackpot for failure.

Of course, some aspects of a role can – and should – stay flexible. But the core of the role, what success looks like and what you actually expect from the person you hire, are all things *you* need to define upfront.

Many managers see filling out a hiring brief as a pointless and boring admin task and pass it off to a recruiter. Big mistake! The hiring brief isn't just paperwork for recruiters – it's a test of the hiring manager's clarity and awareness about what they are looking for.

Many managers are convinced they know exactly who they're looking for. But if you ask them to define clearly what this person will be doing in six months' time and how their success will be measured, you'll often get: *'Well... we'll figure it out as we go.'*

This isn't just about filling in a form. Without a clear idea of who you're hiring and why, the whole process starts to fall apart. Recruiters end up bringing in candidates who aren't quite right – because they were never given a clear brief in the first place. Once hired, the new person is left trying to figure out what's actually expected of them. And six months down the line, frustration kicks in. The manager is unhappy, the new hire feels lost, and yet no one can quite pinpoint where it all went wrong.

How do you know your hiring brief is right? Let's test it with an example.

Imagine you're hiring a junior analyst. Here's what a vague hiring brief might look like:

> *'Looking for a junior analyst. The ideal candidate is detail-oriented, comfortable working in a fast-paced environment*

and able to collaborate across departments. Strong analytical skills required, experience with external databases is a plus.'

What's wrong with this? It's so broad that you could shortlist dozens of candidates but none of them might actually be right for you. There are no clear objectives, no defined success metrics. And in today's world – where more than half of CVs are written with generative AI and stuffed with identical buzzwords – a hiring brief like this turns recruitment into a random matching game, where vague job descriptions meet equally vague résumés.

Now, compare it to a brief that provides clear criteria without turning the search into a hunt for a purple unicorn:

Title: Junior Analyst.
Main Objective:
Increase the efficiency of the analytics team by 30 per cent through external databases and AI-driven tools. Develop a structured approach to working with external providers to ensure seamless data operations.

Expected Results (by the end of the year):
- Increase reporting efficiency – the team should be producing 30 per cent more analytical reports (four per month).
- Develop and implement a dashboard to aggregate external data and provide actionable insights.
- Test at least one AI-driven solution to improve report accuracy.

Who We're Looking For:
- Hard skills: SQL, Python (or R), experience with BI tools.
- Soft skills: can make sense of unstructured data and turn chaos into insights. Thinks beyond tasks – constantly looks for ways to improve processes. Can explain complex ideas in simple terms
- Balances confidence with openness – contributes ideas while

valuing others' perspectives. Works well with different types of people and knows when to listen.

This brief doesn't demand perfection in every area – but it makes it clear what truly matters. We're not looking for a mythical analyst who already knows every tool and methodology. We need someone who can take on clear, tangible challenges, isn't afraid to experiment and test ideas and instinctively tunes in to the people around them – knowing when to share, when to listen and when to lift others up.

If you want to test your hiring brief, simply ask yourself three questions:

What will this person actually *do*?
How will you know they're doing it well?
What specific skills, perspectives or experiences does this candidate bring that directly address the team's current challenges or gaps?

A hiring brief isn't just a formality. It's the foundation that will either help you find the right person or set you up for a cycle of compromises and frustration.

Mistake 2: Hiring on your own

Manager-driven hiring – where the hiring manager oversees the entire process from start to finish – is a common and perfectly valid approach. But I genuinely believe that hiring on your own is a mistake. Why? Because no matter how experienced or self-aware we are, we all have biases.

It's easy to assume that we're objective, especially if we pride ourselves on being open-minded and well educated. But the truth is, bias isn't something we can just switch off – it's part of how our brains work. And while we may not be able to eliminate it entirely, we can certainly minimise its influence when hiring. That's why having a recruitment panel is so important.

Yes, involving a panel can make the hiring process a little longer and sometimes lead to differing opinions – your colleagues might even challenge your perspective. That's actually a good thing. When carefully put together, a panel brings in different viewpoints and helps you make a more balanced, well-informed decision.

Ideally, your panel should include three to five colleagues from different teams, with a mix of experience and backgrounds. Each panel member can focus on different aspects during the interviews – for example: role-specific knowledge, leadership potential or cultural fit (which also gives you a chance to assess both skills and potential, as we discussed earlier). The benefit? A range of perspectives that help reduce bias and lead to stronger hiring choices.

In other words, a panel doesn't just help you find a great candidate – it also prevents you from making a choice based on personal preferences. Like choosing someone because they went to the same university as you and also happen to love Taylor Swift. Or, on the flip side, dismissing someone because they have blue hair and hypnotic nails – which, I must admit, almost happened to me once, until the panel convinced me otherwise. And it turned out to be a brilliant hire!

A small but important detail: ask panel members to keep their thoughts to themselves during the interviews and share them only later in a dedicated discussion. This helps everyone form their own impressions first and leads to a fairer, more thoughtful decision.

Mistake 3: Turning an interview into small talk

Interviews will never be a perfect way to get to know someone – it's impossible in sixty minutes. But for now, it's the only way we have before we start working together and trusting them with important decisions.

So, make the most of that time! You may not get their full story but it's more than enough to understand what drives them and what they value.

All it really takes is some preparation before the interview and actually paying attention during it. Sounds simple enough. And yet, plenty of hiring managers skip both.

How many times have I heard, *'The only way to pick the right person is to trust your gut!'*?

In reality, gut feeling is just bias in disguise. It either whispers to a new manager, *'Hire someone like you – after all, you're great, so how could that possibly go wrong?'*

Or it goes, *'They worked at legendary company X/studied at prestigious university Y, so obviously, they must be amazing!'*

Or sometimes, it takes on an even more desperate tone: *'I've been searching for so long – I need this candidate to be The One.'*

And just like that, decisions get made for all the wrong reasons. The other extreme is hiring someone who *ticks all the boxes*. That approach is a dangerous trap. One of my clients once told me that, at the end of a probation period, he had to let someone go with the words: *'Looks like I hired your CV, not you.'* And that was the best-case scenario – at least the mistake was caught early. More often, a bad hire lingers for years before the problem is finally addressed.

So, during the interview (or ideally, a series of them), your job is to figure out:

1. What from their past experience will help them in this role?

And by experience, I don't just mean having worked in the same industry or holding a similar job title previously. It could be skills, insights or problem-solving approaches they've picked up from work, studies or life in general – anything that can be applied to this role.

A key point: when discussing their achievements, make sure they back up their words with real evidence – facts, figures and concrete examples. If a candidate is all about big claims but can't provide any proof, that's a red flag.

That said, don't dismiss someone just because they come from a completely different field. If they've done their homework, understood the context of the role and your company and can clearly articulate how they'll add value, that's often a far better hire than an industry veteran who shows up asking *you* to explain what your company does.

Motivation and genuine interest in the role are among the strongest predictors of success. You want to know what truly drives the person sitting in front of you. As Warren Buffett once put it in a media interview: *'I've always tried to hire people who love the business more than they love the money.'* And honestly, that's as good a hiring criterion as any.

2. Their potential for growth

Assess their adaptability, critical thinking, emotional maturity, sense of responsibility and approach to problem-solving – along with one other crucial factor: the ability and willingness to learn. Technical skills can always be acquired but a growth mindset is what will ultimately determine whether hiring this person turns out to be one of your best decisions.

If a candidate claims to be responsible or highly adaptable or a fast learner – what's the story that proves it? Don't hesitate to ask follow-up questions until you're certain you understand what they actually mean – don't settle for vague statements, buzzwords, hyperbolic claims or corporate fluff.

3. Their emotional intelligence and ability to work in a team

Look for how they relate to others. Self-awareness, empathy, emotional maturity – and just as importantly, how they respond to change and uncertainty. These qualities can be tricky to assess, especially with experienced candidates who know how to give polished answers or second-guess what you want to hear. That's why careful listening and observation are key. Here, it's not just about what they say, but how they say it.

How do they talk about themselves, their colleagues, their current and former boss? Do they take full credit for successes while subtly blaming others for setbacks? Do they speak with respect, or is there a trace of bitterness or condescension?

Avoid generic questions like *'How do you handle conflict?'* – chances are, you'll get a textbook answer about open communication and compromise, which won't tell you much. Instead, ask questions that reveal their values and instincts. Try something unexpected that encourages them to drop the script and show you how they really think.

Here are some of the questions I personally use to get a glimpse of the real person behind the polished interview answers:

'Do you consider yourself lucky?'
This question helps reveal whether the candidate has a sense of gratitude – towards themselves, others and their circumstances. Are they naturally optimistic or do they focus more on setbacks and obstacles? Their answers can give insight into their overall mindset.

'What's a compliment you've received that has really stayed with you?'
People tend to remember compliments that align with their self-image or reflect the qualities they most take pride in. Their response can give you a glimpse into what truly matters to them and what kind of recognition they value.

'If you could give your two-years-ago self one piece of advice, what would it be?'
While their answer might focus on career choices or education rather than emotional intelligence, the way they reflect on their past decisions – and the words they choose – can tell you a lot about their self-

MISSION 4: TURN YOUR TEAM INTO YOUR BIGGEST PROJECT

awareness, growth mindset and ability to learn from experience.

'If I gave you one minute to teach me something new, what would it be?'
This is a great way to lighten the mood while getting a glimpse into the person behind the CV. What will they choose? And, more importantly, *how* will they go about teaching it?

'What will your boss, colleagues and team say about you – when we call and ask?'
I borrowed this brilliant question from the book *Who: The A Method for Hiring* by Geoff Smart and Randy Street. The key here is in the wording: *when* we call and ask. This phrasing shifts the candidate's mindset, making it harder for them to rely on wishful thinking.

'Name three people you admire and give three reasons for each.'
At first, candidates may stick to standard, socially acceptable answers. But as the conversation unfolds, you'll quickly start to see what they truly value and where their priorities lie.

And here's an unexpected question a recruiter friend once shared with me:

'How would you describe your driving?'
At first, I laughed. But then I realised – it actually works. A person's driving style can tell you a surprising amount about them.

Please, make sure to leave time for the candidate to ask questions. What they ask can tell you a lot – what interests them, how well they understand your company and what really matters to them in a role.

And while we're talking about respect and decency, don't ghost candidates who don't make it through. In today's overcrowded job market, it's become far too common, but that doesn't make it right. A quick follow-up is a simple way to show professionalism – and it says as much about you and your company as the hiring process itself. Your attitude towards people shouldn't stop at those already on your payroll.

Letting people go – the cost of hesitation

Hiring strong people is tough. But letting go of those who aren't pulling their weight? That's even harder. And that's exactly why so many managers put it off for as long as possible. But if you're serious about building a strong team, you have to learn to do both.

The simplest way to make this easier – for yourself and for your team – is to get hiring right from the start. If you bring in strong, non-toxic people, both performance and trust will naturally set the right standard.

Let's say you're already on that path – you've hired some strong players. But at the same time, you're hesitating when it comes to the weaker ones. That's completely natural for new managers. You want to do the right thing, avoid mistakes and still be seen as a good person – both by your team and by yourself.

Unfortunately, that kind of hesitation is just avoidance – and it comes at a cost.

A team isn't just a collection of individuals; it's a dynamic system. Add strong people and the system gets stronger. Leave weak or unmotivated ones in place, and the whole team will inevitably start to drag. Hiring is a crucial step but if you want to build a truly strong team, it's not just about who you bring in – it's also about who you're willing to let go.

I've seen it happen more than once: strong players leaving not because of low salaries or bad conditions but because they were tired of carrying teammates who weren't willing – or able – to keep up. A weak performer isn't the real issue. The real issue is a manager who's afraid to do something about it. And the cost isn't just losing your best people – it's failing to attract new ones. Top performers don't want to join a team of mediocrity.

It's your responsibility to act decisively – and fast. The first step is understanding exactly what, or rather who, you're dealing with.

Chances are, underperformers in your team both frustrate and disappoint you. But letting emotions take over won't help – it only makes it harder to see the situation clearly.

I've been there myself, until I realised that frustration often comes from seeing the team as an extension of yourself. You assume they should just get it, that what's obvious to you must be obvious to them. *How can they not understand something so simple?* And that frustration feels almost like your own arm or leg refusing to follow a command from your brain.

But that's not how it works with other people. Your team isn't an extension of you and the first step is learning to separate yourself from them. The ability to see things from someone else's perspective isn't just a useful skill – it's a mark of a mature leader.

So, you need to figure out two things: WHAT isn't happening that you expect to happen, and WHY it isn't happening.

The first part is about your own self-reflection – you need to define it clearly for yourself before anything else. Not just *'they're underperforming', 'they're not keeping up'* or *'the client is unhappy'* but specifically: What *exactly* isn't happening? What's *missing*?

The second part – the *why* – requires more than just your own conclusions. You need to ask open-ended questions and try to understand the other person's perspective. And these questions need to be truly open and neutral.

For example: *'What was behind that decision?'* or *'How did you arrive at that conclusion?'*

Rather than: *'Don't you realise how important this is to us?'* or *'Why did you let the team down?'*

Sometimes, the explanation is much simpler than you think. Remember Dan, whose story I shared in Mission 2? He had just lost his dog and was struggling with grief but instead of support, he got a blunt reproach about his attitude. Before you take the next step, make sure you've genuinely understood the situation. There could be all sorts of reasons behind what's happening.

Most companies have a standard protocol for dealing with low performers but in my view, there are two distinct types – and they need to be handled in completely different ways.

Strugglers. These are people who have blind spots – either about what's expected of them in their role, about their own skill gaps or even about where their natural strengths truly lie. In other words, they *want* to do better but for one reason or another they *can't*.

Your strategy: give them support.

They need tools, training, coaching – or in some cases, help discovering and using their natural strengths (check out tests like StrengthsFinder) so they can consider a role change. You've probably seen or heard stories of people who completely thrived after switching roles – sometimes in ways no one expected. A friend of mine left a 'creative' marketing job for logistics. One of my clients quit digital ad sales to open a restaurant. And you might have come across that viral LinkedIn profile of someone who left Morgan Stanley after ten years to become a goose farmer.

The key here is clarity – both you and your team member need to be on the same page about what's expected in their role. This makes everything easier. Either they improve their performance, which is absolutely possible, or they move into a role where they *do* thrive. Whichever way it goes, helping them find their way forward is one of the most rewarding things you can do as a manager.

Loafers are employees who *could* perform better but *choose* not to. They put in less effort, either because they feel undervalued or believe that their lack of contribution goes unnoticed. This is known as the *Ringelmann effect*, which describes how people working in a group tend to put in less effort than they would individually – like in a tug-of-war, where the more people are pulling, the less force each individual applies.

In a team, these people do just enough to get by, yet often feel they deserve more. They're rarely confused about what's expected of them – they know the rules but choose to ignore them because they are simply not motivated. Many have been with the company for years and feel overlooked despite their early contributions. Others have simply lost interest in their role but, for one reason or another, aren't ready to move on.

Some people really know how to game the system. I had a colleague managing a client in California from our office in Europe who always strolled into the office late, after lunch – claiming he worked into the night to match their time zone. It sounded reasonable. Until the client casually mentioned that their account manager was never available. Turns out, while he told us he was working late, he told them he was logging off early because he'd been working since early morning. Impressive time-zone acrobatics! Aka, lying.

Why are 'loafers' so damaging? They undermine the team's sense of fairness. When others are working hard while their manager tolerates loafing, frustration sets in. This behaviour is demotivating, and worse – it's contagious.

Your strategy: give them a choice.

Once you've understood the root cause of their low motivation, it's time to be clear: they have a choice. Either they step up, change their attitude and meet expectations (ideally exceeding them), or they move on.

Whatever strategy you choose, set a clear deadline for improvement – and make sure both of you are aligned on what needs to change. Write it down. What does 'getting better' actually look like? What will you be looking for?

It's tempting to give someone more time and hope things will work out. But waiting too long doesn't help them and it certainly doesn't help the team. Ideally it should be sixty days, ninety at the very most.

And don't just set a date – schedule check-ins along the way, so your final conversation doesn't come as a surprise.

If they turn things around – acknowledge it! Don't just nod and move on. Reinforce what's good and celebrate it. But if nothing changes, don't hesitate. Make the decision and act.

Most of the time, firing happens too late. And no matter how experienced you are, it's never easy. Guilt, the fear of being 'the bad guy' or not wanting to seem like a manager who doesn't care – all of this can get in the way. But in the long run, it's always better to make one tough decision than to stay stuck in a situation that drags the whole team down. Firing someone for the first time wasn't easy for me either – until an HR colleague shared an aphorism that stuck with me:

'A horrible end is better than endless horror.'

You can spend forever trying to save someone, but the team won't stand still. The strongest will move on. Those with potential will never reach it. Your hesitation won't work miracles – it will only keep the whole team stuck in a state of mediocrity.

It's not about being a good guy or a bad guy. It's about stepping up for the people who are willing and capable – because they're the ones who deserve a strong team around them.

MISSION 5:

Expand your playing field

Have you ever wondered what really sets apart new managers from those who've mastered the role? It's not just about experience – it's about how they see the bigger picture and where they choose to direct their efforts.

The best managers don't just zoom in on their own team. They take a broader view, seeing beyond immediate tasks to understand how they can help steer the business as a whole. They develop the kind of thinking that CEOs rely on – not to chase a title but to drive impact and grow beyond their current role.

New managers often find themselves caught up in managing tasks and keeping everything under control. They focus on what needs to be done *right now*, making sure things run smoothly. But at some point, just keeping up isn't enough.

The shift happens when you stop seeing your team as a separate island and start noticing how it connects with the rest of the company. Decisions made elsewhere will affect your team – and the way you position your team will, in turn, influence the business.

For seasoned managers, this comes naturally. Instead of getting lost in the day-to-day, they pay attention to how people, teams and processes fit together. They remove obstacles, strengthen connections and create momentum. They're able to do this because they manage complexity – allowing them to lead people, rather than just oversee the work.

In previous chapters, we talked about building teams, delegating, and developing people – all of which are crucial. But as you move up, the challenge becomes bigger. Management is no longer just about running your team efficiently – it's about stepping into a broader playing field, where you need to understand how departments collaborate, how resources are allocated and how to position your team for success.

This shift doesn't happen overnight. It requires three core skills that will set you apart:

1. **System thinking** will help you understand how different teams are connected, why certain problems keep coming back and what really shapes the way things work – not just in your team but across the company (or even the industry).
2. **Strategic thinking** is about making deliberate choices – deciding where to invest your time and effort so you're not just busy but actually moving in the right direction.
3. **Political intelligence** will help you understand how people's decisions are formed, notice *unspoken* dynamics and build the right connections to get things done.

There's no point at which you can say, 'I've completely mastered these areas.' They're not something you can tick off a list – they're dimensions of development that require constant attention and growth. But the more you understand them, the better equipped you are to handle complexity with confidence.

Let's take a closer look at each of them.

System thinking

When a chess grandmaster looks at the board, they don't just see individual pieces. They see how everything connects – opportunities, risks and the way the game is unfolding. They recognise patterns, anticipate moves and *shape* the game rather than simply reacting to it.

It's no different in business. Managers who only focus on immediate problems find themselves constantly firefighting. But those

MISSION 5: EXPAND YOUR PLAYING FIELD

who look beyond their own team – who understand how different departments interact – can see challenges before they escalate, position their team for success and influence decisions instead of just responding to them.

System thinking is about recognising patterns and hidden connections. It helps you spot why certain problems keep coming back and how small shifts in one area can trigger a much bigger effect across the company. It's not just about understanding complexity – it's about thinking like a leader.

So don't make decisions in isolation. Consider ripple effects, competing priorities and the long-term impact of your choices. The earlier you start thinking this way, the more effective you become – not just in solving today's problems but in building what's ahead.

- What decisions outside my team affect our work the most?
  (If a major shift happens elsewhere in the company – will we be prepared or will we just have to deal with the consequences?)
- Where do bottlenecks happen between teams?
  (Are these just occasional slowdowns or do they point to deeper issues in how teams collaborate?)
- What patterns keep repeating, despite efforts to fix them?
  (Are we tackling the symptoms instead of the root cause? If the same issues keep resurfacing, what's driving them?)
- What's changing in the company or industry that could affect us in six months?
  (Are we making moves based only on today's reality – or setting ourselves up for what's coming next?)

You don't need to map out the entire organisation. But simply noticing a few key patterns can help you anticipate problems, make smarter choices and be proactive rather than reactive.

This system thinking ability becomes especially useful when

you're dealing with competing priorities inside the company.

Imagine you're leading a marketing team, and you need approval for a budget to hire a top-tier photographer. The goal? To improve brand perception and ultimately drive sales. It seems like a straightforward call – until procurement pushes back. Their KPI isn't brand value or revenue growth – it's cost saving. They argue that a cheaper photographer will do just fine.

Without system thinking, this turns into a frustrating battle. You fight for quality; they fight for savings. But let's take a step back.

The real issue isn't just this photoshoot. It's about how decisions are made across teams with different KPIs – and how they all connect to the company's P&L. If procurement focuses only on cutting costs and marketing focuses only on brand impact, who is looking at the bigger picture?

Instead of arguing, you can find ways to align goals. Maybe you show procurement data on how high-quality visuals improve conversion rates. Maybe you involve leadership to ensure that cost-saving targets don't come at the expense of brand value. Maybe you adjust procurement guidelines so that marketing investments aren't evaluated purely on price.

System thinking helps you move from friction to influence. Instead of getting stuck in departmental conflicts, you start noticing how things are linked – and use that to make smarter moves.

But recognising the wider context is only part of the equation. You also need to shift perspectives – to see decisions the way those above you see them.

Here's a thinking trick that a colleague of mine, who rose through the ranks from assistant to senior VP, shared with me. When tackling problems or analysing a situation, he would always ask himself this important question:

> 'If I were in my boss's position, how would I see this? What about the boss above them? What about the CEO?'

He called it *level-up thinking* and before long, it became second nature. It didn't just help him make better decisions – it played a huge role in how his team grew. He encouraged his people to see things not just from their own point of view but from the perspective of those making the final call.

The result? His team didn't just follow what was happening – they started anticipating the next move. They adapted more quickly, thought ahead and acted with more confidence.

By combining system thinking and level-up thinking, you stop reacting to the game – you start changing it.

Strategic thinking

Strategic thinking is one of the most sought-after and admired qualities in managers – it needs no extra PR. The higher you climb, the more it becomes the defining skill that separates those who simply keep things running smoothly from those who create real impact. Senior leaders don't just execute plans – they decide where to invest, which battles to fight and what risks are worth taking. But strategy isn't just for the C-suite. Even at a team level, the choices you make shape long-term results. Whether it's deciding how to allocate your team's time, which projects to prioritise or how to position your work within the company, you're already making strategic choices – whether consciously or not.

Many managers believe they're engaging in strategic planning but somehow, the strategic part quietly fades into the background, leaving just... planning. What actions need to be taken? What resources are required? How long will it take? These are all important questions – but they belong to the *implementation* stage. Planning is crucial for executing a strategy, but it comes *after* strategy, not instead of it. This is the stage where you define and align OKRs and an action plan. Whether it's about enhancing customer experience, launching a new flavour or developing a loyalty programme – this is planning, not strategy.

Why does strategy often get overlooked? Simply put, many people don't actually understand what it is. Strategy isn't about making endless planning lists – it's about making choices.

It answers two fundamental questions:[2]

1. **Where do we play?** What products do we focus on? Which customers do we serve? Which markets, geographies and channels do we commit to? And just as importantly – where *don't* we play?
2. **How do we win?** What's our competitive edge? What's our unique value proposition? Why should customers choose us over others?

This approach applies at every level – whether you're leading a team, a department or an entire company.

Imagine you're leading a sales team. You're consistently hitting targets but your best performers are spending too much time on small accounts. You have a choice: keep things as they are (and risk stagnation) or shift focus. Should your team prioritise high-value clients? Should you create a dedicated team for small accounts? Should you invest in self-serve tools so your team can spend more time on complex deals?

Or take a product manager launching a new feature. Do you release a basic version quickly to test demand or invest time in building a fully polished product? Do you centre your efforts on your existing customer base or use this as a way to break into a new market?

This is strategy: choosing where to play (enterprise clients vs. mass market, quick launch vs. long-term development) and how to win (dedicated teams, automation scaling existing users vs. expanding into new markets).

---

[2] This framing of strategy (Where do we play? How do we win?) was popularised by A.G. Lafley and Roger L. Martin in their book *Playing to Win*.

The hardest part is that strategy is also about saying *no*. You can't be everything to everyone. Making a strategic choice means placing a bet on something – and taking on the risk that comes with it.

For many managers, especially in large corporations, taking a risk feels almost existential. Planning feels safe. When you're making a plan, you're working with known variables – activities, resources, timelines – things that (at least in theory) are within your control. Strategy, however, deals with the *unknown*. Its ultimate success depends on external factors – on whether customers actually choose your product or service over the competition. And that's never guaranteed.

That's why many managers unconsciously (or very consciously) avoid making real strategic choices. Instead, they opt for risk-free 'strategies', which are either familiar paths that have been tested before, overly broad approaches that try to cover all bases or a set of vague, generic initiatives that look busy but don't make hard trade-offs.

This kind of imitation – doing things because they *seem* strategic rather than because they *are* – is just another form of the cargo cult thinking we've discussed before.

If you want big results, you have to take a bet.

There's no great outcome without risk. As the saying goes, *who dares, wins*. Real strategy means embracing uncertainty and owning your bet. It means choosing a direction, committing to it and doing everything in your power to execute it.

Of course, that doesn't mean betting blindly. Good strategists aren't reckless – they manage risk. The goal isn't just to place big bets but also to stay flexible, adjust when needed and know when to pivot or abandon a failing strategy.

So how do you navigate uncertainty instead of just reacting to it?

1. **Keep it simple.** Overcomplicated strategies don't work. Break your strategy into clear, logical blocks that can be evaluated separately. That way, if something isn't working, you can adjust

individual elements rather than starting from scratch. Don't hesitate to test your thinking and your logic with the generative AI platform of your choice: it will help as an impartial partner.

2. **Prototype and test.** Don't spend years perfecting a strategy before trying it out. Use *fast validation* – small-scale pilots, MVPs (minimum viable product) and experiment. If something fails, let it fail *fast* so you can move on.
3. **Use scenario planning.** This is where things get tricky. For such a basic concept – *think ahead about different possible outcomes* – scenario planning faces an enormous amount of psychological resistance.

Not just in business – people avoid it in everyday life, too. One of my friends refuses to keep even basic medicine at home because he's afraid that if he buys it, he'll jinx himself and immediately get ill. Another friend didn't sign a pre-nup contract because *'We're not planning to get divorced.'* And at work, I once heard someone say, *'If we include a backup plan for this project, leadership will think we don't believe in success.'*

Our brains are wired to avoid discomfort, especially when it comes to potential threats or failures. Sometimes, this even spills into 'magical thinking' – *if I don't acknowledge the bad outcome, it won't happen.*

But the truth is, the world is unpredictable. Unexpected things *will* happen. It's not only about how your strategy and planning work. There could be an economic downturn, a regulatory change or an industry shift that no one saw coming. Scenario planning isn't about pessimism – it's about being *prepared*.

Be a smart player; always have three scenarios:

1. A worst-case scenario (e.g., revenue drops completely).
2. A moderate downside (e.g., a 50 per cent drop).

3.   A mild setback (e.g., slight decline but manageable).

Adjust these for your specific situation – whether it's market conditions, customer behaviour or any other key variable. The point isn't to predict the future perfectly. It's to give yourself and your team the best possible odds of winning, no matter what happens.

Political intelligence

Navigating politics is an art and it takes more than just sharp thinking – whether it's system thinking or strategic thinking. You'll also need emotional intelligence, empathy, keen observation skills and the ability to truly listen: to 'read between the lines' and spot the layers of motivation driving other people's actions.

No matter how brilliant your strategy is, no matter how well you analyse the system, if you ignore the human dynamics – people's influence, hidden power structures, hidden agendas and shifting relationships – you'll eventually find yourself on the losing side.

Political games and power struggles have existed for as long as humanity itself. Throughout history, those in power – whether tribal leaders, emperors, high priests or military commanders – have been at the centre of intricate relationships, shifting alliances and fierce rivalries. In the modern world, these dynamics haven't disappeared – they've simply found new arenas. Beyond global politics, we now see corporate strategies, internal power plays and boardroom manoeuvres shaping organisations and careers.

There's no escaping workplace politics. Even if your company has just ten people, politics are still at play. Wherever there are people, you'll find conflicting interests, power plays, alliances, resource trading and informal influence.

Navigating politics doesn't mean becoming manipulative or scheming. It's about understanding how power and influence actually work. Senior leaders don't just react to information; they weigh who it's coming from, what the underlying agenda might be and how it fits into the bigger picture. The better you understand this, the better you can position yourself and your team to be heard at the right level.

Everyone knows that managing up and sideways and making your team's work visible matter – but few actually put in the effort consistently.

Some people believe that good work speaks for itself – but that's a big mistake. How well people in your organisation know about your team's work is just as important as the work itself. Your team's success doesn't just build your reputation – it also strengthens your boss's position. And that, in turn, means more trust, resources and opportunities coming your way.

Others struggle to build relationships with senior leaders simply because they doubt themselves.

One of my clients, despite leading a large team, still felt like a little girl in front of senior leadership. She doubted herself, hesitated to talk about her achievements and often heard that she lacked visibility. The way she saw herself – as a mortal speaking to gods – shaped how others saw her too, through both her words and behaviour.

Another client had the opposite issue – she looked down on upper management. In her case, the company founders made odd decisions, ignored logic and, in her view, were simply not competent enough. As a result, every interaction with them carried a defensive, almost combative tone.

If we strip it down, these are 'student' versus 'teacher' perspectives. The first feels like they're never experienced enough and are afraid of making mistakes. The second assumes they're the smartest in the room and underestimates everyone else. Neither helps in building healthy work relationships.

As we've discussed before, like it or not, we often project parental roles onto our bosses. Just as children react to parents in different ways – some seeking approval, others rebelling and some withdrawing altogether – employees mirror these patterns in their relationships with senior leaders. Some take the *student* role, looking up to their boss and doubting their own authority. Others adopt the *teacher* stance, dismissing leadership as incompetent and positioning themselves as the only rational voice in the room. But once you stop seeing leadership as either infallible or incompetent and start recognising them as just people – with their own strengths, weaknesses, interests and vulnerabilities – working with them becomes much less complicated and far more productive.

Since your team's success, the promotion of your ideas or even solving structural challenges depends on building relationships with key people – both inside and outside your company – it makes sense to create a stakeholder map.

But not just any stakeholder map – the kind that's more than just a list of people you occasionally invite for coffee or find excuses to meet. You need one that will actually help you in the long run.

To do this, you need to go beyond simply identifying the obvious stakeholders – the ones directly linked to your team's success, like the head of marketing, the analytics lead or the procurement director.

You also need to think about who your key decision-maker actually listens to? Who's known as the company's go-to early adopter, always open to unconventional ideas? Who, on the other hand, blindly follows protocols and brand manuals, no matter the situation? Whose opinion still holds weight – even if they're already one foot out the door, enjoying their garden leave?

To map this out, you can break stakeholders down based on their potential influence on your plan:

- Decision-makers – the ones who make the key calls.
- Influencers – those who don't have formal authority but can still have a big say in the outcome.
- Connectors – the people who can get you to the right people.
- Blockers – those who might slow things down or stand in your way.

How can you use this map? Think of it as a way to build momentum for your ideas or tackle challenges step by step. Instead of trying to go straight to the top, start with those who can help you lay the groundwork.

Pay attention to people's interests, motivations, goals and vulnerabilities – and don't assume everyone sees things the way you do. Even if everyone in your company proudly champions increasing shareholder value, people still have their own motivations – shaped by their roles, teams and personal ambitions.

The better you understand who's who on the way to your goal, the easier it is to plan your next move. Here's a simple example:

'I need to push forward a new idea. Instead of going straight to Jim – the guy who nods but never commits – I start with Tom and Jane, who have his ear. If they're on board, Jim will miraculously find the idea "very interesting". Meanwhile, my team works on winning over marketing because if they don't see what's in it for them, they'll pretend they never got the memo. Their boss, Brian, is another story – he says no to everything on principle but once he sees that everyone else is on board, he'll suddenly claim it was his idea all along. By the time we present to Jessica, the CEO, the leadership team is already on board.'

This is how decisions are really made in organisations. It's not always a logical, linear process!

And as you build your plan, don't overplay it by ignoring your manager. Their interests matter too. Make sure they look good and stay in the limelight.

Yes, even if you secretly suspect they rather enjoy that limelight a bit too much.

Your manager isn't just an obstacle to be worked around or a ceiling on your autonomy. Just like you, they're navigating their own pressures – expectations from above, shifting priorities, political

MISSION 5: EXPAND YOUR PLAYING FIELD

crosswinds and the ever-present risk of being thrown under the bus.

You want your team to understand your context, right? Well, extend the same courtesy upwards. Try to understand theirs – and where possible, help your team see it too. The stronger the trust and alignment between you and your manager, the more powerful your position becomes.

I know – it's not always easy to see them as a 'partner'. But think of it this way: when you help your manager shine, it reflects well on you too. Their success becomes your buffer, your runway, your reputation-by-association. A credible, confident manager gives you room to move, to experiment, to lead. A manager on shaky ground, on the other hand, is far more likely to second-guess every move – and guess who gets micromanaged in the process?

And if you ever feel the urge to prove just how much sharper, bolder or more visionary you are – please pause. The impulse to outshine your manager rarely leads where you think it will. Even if you do win a round or two, it's unlikely you'll win the whole war. The moment you try to be 'the real leader in the room', don't be surprised if your manager feels the urge to reassert control. It's a very human reaction.

And history, as always, has its cautionary examples. Stealing the stage, as it turns out, rarely ends well. Consider Nicolas Fouquet, the ambitious French finance minister who made one crucial mistake: he dazzled the king.

His biggest misstep? Hosting an extravagant party at his newly built Château de Vaux-le-Vicomte in 1661, which was far grander than anything Louis XIV owned at the time.

The king saw it as an unforgivable display of wealth and power. Soon after, Fouquet was arrested by D'Artagnan (yes, that one!), put on trial for embezzlement and sentenced to life in prison.

All the development areas we've reviewed – seeing connections, making strategic moves and navigating workplace politics – only make sense if you apply them in the real world. *Constantly challenging yourself to think big, consider the world outside your immediate perimeter and take into account people's interests and dynamics is the key to playing at a different level.*

But there's a catch: you can't really apply these skills if your mindset is locked in survival mode. And survival mode doesn't always look like a crisis. More often, it means falling into patterns that feel like the 'right' way to operate as a manager but actually limit your perspective.

Here are four of the most common traps that keep managers from stepping up and seeing the bigger picture.

The most common traps that hold you back
DEFENSIVE MINDSET

When faced with uncertainty, some managers instinctively go into protection mode, focusing all their energy on shielding their team from external pressures. They become hyper-alert to risks, resist change and start seeing senior leadership as a threat rather than an ally. Other teams stop looking like partners and start feeling like competitors.

Instead of leading, they dig in, reinforcing a siege mentality – closing ranks, guarding their territory and preparing for battle rather than collaboration. The us-versus-them mindset takes hold. Their team rallies around them but at a cost – trust erodes, collaboration suffers and opportunities to influence the broader conversation slip away.

'If we don't stand our ground, they'll walk all over us.'

'Another ridiculous decision from the top... How can they not see what's right in front of them?'

'We need to stick together – they're piling on the pressure again.'

CONTROL MINDSET

For some managers, uncertainty feels like chaos and their natural response is to tighten their grip. They get involved in every detail, checking, approving and overseeing everything to make sure nothing goes wrong. At first, this can feel like responsible leadership – staying on top of things, ensuring quality, preventing mistakes. But soon, it turns into micromanagement.

One of the hardest things for managers with this mindset is letting go – not just of tasks but of access to information and decision-making. They hesitate to let their team interact directly with senior leaders or cross-functional teams, fearing misalignment, loss of control or simply being left out of the loop.

'I can't trust them with major responsibilities – they're just not ready.'

'I need to see every email, presentation and report before it's sent.'

'If everyone starts making their own arrangements, it'll be chaos.'

Ironically, the more they try to control and micromanage, the more they slow things down – and the less their team learns to operate independently.

ISOLATION MINDSET

Some managers fall into the trap of believing they're the only ones truly working. Deep down, they question their own competence – but instead of acknowledging it, they convince themselves that others simply aren't reliable enough. If they delegate too much, what if people start wondering what they actually do?

So, they take on more than they should, convinced the team can't handle it without them. They delegate only the most routine tasks – and even then, with painstaking instructions. Outwardly, they assure others they trust their team, but their actions say otherwise.

'If you want something done right, do it yourself.'

'It's all down to me.'

'Other departments are all talk – they just slow things down.'

What starts as a way to ensure things get done properly ends up creating bottlenecks, stalling progress and leaving the manager feeling exhausted and isolated.

Tactical mindset

With endless demands and constant pressure, it's easy for managers to get stuck in firefighting mode – solving problems as they arise, focusing on immediate tasks and never finding time to step back and think strategically.

When everything feels urgent, bigger-picture thinking gets pushed aside. The manager and their team spend all their time reacting instead of planning, handling today's crisis while unknowingly setting themselves up for tomorrow's.

'I've got no time to think about strategy.'
'My job is to keep things ticking over.'
'If I don't sort this now, it'll just get worse.'

At first, it feels productive – after all, they're constantly busy, solving problems. But over time, this cycle leads to burnout, stagnation and a lack of real progress.

All these thinking traps – the defensive mindset, the need for control, the tendency to isolate, the pull towards firefighting – ultimately serve the same purpose: they create a sense of security. They keep you safe, anchored in the familiar and shielded from uncertainty. And in this mode, you can survive. You can keep things running, minimise risk and make sure nothing falls apart.

Spoiler alert: playing not to lose is not the same as playing to win.

If your focus is purely on maintaining control, avoiding mistakes and protecting what you have, you'll stay afloat – but you won't move forward. Instead of staying ahead, you'll end up reacting, protecting the team and relying on ready-made solutions. This brings us back to cargo cult thinking – imitating rather than truly understanding and taking control. You'll get better at managing today's reality, but you won't shape what happens next.

And the biggest mistake? Believing that your ability to see the bigger picture depends on the company you work for, the culture around you or whether leadership 'allows' you to step up. It doesn't.

MISSION 5: EXPAND YOUR PLAYING FIELD

First and foremost, recognise that uncertainty isn't a threat – it's a constant. Your brain may treat workplace challenges as if they are life-or-death situations but in reality, no one is about to throw you into a cage with a tiger. Even in the worst-case scenario – failing publicly or even losing your job – life goes on. The real risk is getting stuck in a small, defensive mindset that limits your growth.

So, what's the alternative?

- Shift your focus from avoiding risks to learning how to navigate them. Growth comes from movement, not from standing still.
- Reframe your thinking – instead of 'I must not get this wrong,' ask yourself, 'What's the smartest move I can make?'
- Let go of the need for certainty. The game is always changing. The sooner you accept that, the faster you can adapt – and lead.

No one is going to hand you a CEO's mindset – you build it yourself. It starts with shifting your perspective from defending your ground to expanding your playing field. It's about stepping beyond your immediate team, understanding the broader system and positioning yourself as someone who doesn't just keep things running but makes things happen.

Think like a senior leader. Act like a senior leader. Not because you want the title, but because the strongest and most daring don't wait for permission to think at the next level. They take ownership of their space – not by reacting to the system but by learning to shape it.

So the real question is: **Will you choose to play it safe or are you ready to step up and play the bigger game – to win?**

Epilogue

If there's one thing new managers mention most often, it's the weight of responsibility. The feeling that everything now depends on you. The pressure to deliver results – not just personally but through your team. It's exciting. It's terrifying. And it's real.

Yes, results do matter. Revenue growth, brand KPIs, a successful product launch, a big contract signed – these are all signs that you're doing something right. But let me ask you this: how do you measure success as a leader beyond the numbers?

At the beginning of my career, I thought leadership was about keeping things under control – hitting targets, making things run smoothly, staying on top of everything. Years later, I realised something crucial: leadership isn't about control. It's about the *ripple effect* you create. And that's something you build every single day, often without even realising it.

One day, you'll take on new challenges and step into new roles. All those projects, all those meetings, the urgent deadlines – all of them will fade into memory. People will move on. You will move on and what you did will be forgotten. *How* you did it is what will be remembered.

Did you stand for something? Did you speak up? Did people see you as a leader worth following – or just another manager delivering the numbers and playing by the book? Did your team feel like they were growing, learning and being challenged? Or did they feel stuck, having to prove themselves constantly in an effort to meet some impossible, invisible standard?

Leadership isn't about a single moment of recognition. It's built in the thousands of small moments where you make choices – how you show up, how you respond, how you lead. Some days will be messy. Others will be brilliant. You will make mistakes. You will doubt yourself. But waiting for the 'perfect moment' to be the leader you want to be? That's not how it works. You start *now*.

So, find your voice. It's one of the rarest things in the corporate world. Too many managers lose themselves in the system – mirroring those above them, following unwritten rules, blending in. Over time, they stop questioning. They stop thinking for themselves.

The best leaders never do that.

They ask questions. They challenge assumptions. They think before they copy. Even if something has worked a hundred times before, they still question whether it will work the hundred-and-first.

Because if you don't challenge yourself, how can you expect to challenge anyone else?

If you haven't done this yet, start today. Write down your managerial philosophy. What do you believe about leadership? About people? About success? What are the values and principles you won't compromise on? How do you want to lead? Then live it. Because when you find your own voice, you give others permission to find theirs.

And that's how real leadership happens. Not by following scripts. Not by falling into the cargo cult and waiting passively for success to land. *But by thinking for yourself – and giving others the courage to do the same.*

Index

adaptation, 41, 42–3
Adorno, Theodor W., 9
AI (Artificial Intelligence), 42–3, 44, 62, 66, 71
Alice in Wonderland (Carroll), 5–6
'anchors', 3
annual performance review, 26, 27
avoidant behaviour, 3

BBDO, 4
BCG Insights (Boston Consulting Group), 47

'cargo cult', 1–2, 7, 42, 43, 44, 89, 98
Carroll, Lewis, 5
Chartered Management Institute, 2
ChatGPT, 9, 34
coaching, 48–51
corporate jargon, 9
corrective feedback, 33–7
   'sandwich' technique, 33
   'strengths-based' approach, 33
Coursera, 45
credibility, 62
crisis of identity, 5–8

D'Artagnan, Charles de Castelmore, Count, 95

De Bono, Edward, 44
delegating, 16–19, 38
   coaching style, 17, 18
   collaborative style, 17
   directive style, 17, 18
   visionary style, 17
difficult conversations *see* corrective feedback
dismissals, 77–82
   hesitation, 78–9

expectations, 52

fast validation, 90
feedback, 25–40
   emotional reactions to, 32–3, 34–5
   encourage vs discourage, 29–31
   see also annual performance review; corrective feedback; fight, flight or freeze; manager evaluations; Second Score
fight, flight or freeze, 25–7
Financial Times, 47
Fouquet, Nicolas, 95
French invasion of Russia (1812), 9

goals setting, 8, 12

INDEX

Gone with the Wind (Mitchell), 26
Google, 4, 13
growth and development, 41–62
   barriers, removal of, 44, 48–9
   books and online resources, 46–7
   coaching, 48–51
   relearning, 44
   roadmaps, 60–1
   self as driver, 62
   sharing knowledge, 47–8
   training and courses, 45
   workshops, 45–6
   see also High Standards & High Support approach; motivation and incentives for growth
growth mindset, 52, 59

Heen, Sheila, 38
High Standards & High Support approach, 52–5
Hogan test, 32
humility, 23, 38, 40

'imposter syndrome', 6
interviews, 73–8
   past experience, 74–5
   potential for growth, 75
   emotional intelligence, 75–8

'karoshi syndrome', 19
keen judgement, 21–2
Khan Academy, 45
Kodak, 42

lack of training, 2–3
Leo Burnett, 4

level-up thinking, 86–7
Louis XIV, King of France, 95

manager evaluations, 37–40
managerial philosophy, 101
Maslow, Abraham, 49
McCann Erickson, 4
McKinsey, 47, 58
measuring success, 100–1
micromanagement, 18–19
Minto, Barbara, 54
motivation/incentives for growth
   company priorities and, 58
   financial, 55–6
   promotions, 55–6
   recognition, 57–8
   reinventing the role, 59–60
   team achievements, 59

Napoleon I, Emperor of the French, 9
Nokia, 42

OKR (Objectives and Key Results), 12–15, 16, 31, 87
OKR International, 13

perfectionism, 20–3
'playing field', expansion of, 83–99
   control mindset, 96–7
   defensive mindset, 96
   isolation mindset, 97
   political intelligence, 84, 91–6
   strategic thinking, 84, 87–91
   system thinking, 84–7
   tactical mindset, 98–9
poor planning, 9–10

predictability, 31–3
  emotions and, 32–3
proactive curiosity, 21
Pyramid Principle (Minto), 54

recruitment, 66–9, 78
  hiring mistakes, 69–74
  panel, 72–3
  see also interviews
resources, 10
responsibility, 100
Ringelmann effect, 80–1
ripple effect, 100
'rivers of thinking', 44

scenario planning, 90
Schmidt, Eric, 66
Second Score, 38
self-awareness, 38
skill gap, 54
Smart, Geoff, 77
stakeholder map, 93–5
'stop phrase', 33
Street, Randy, 77
StrengthsFinder, 80
student role, 93
survival mode, 96

teacher stance, 93
team, 10–12
  as a project, 63–78
  see also delegating; dismissals; feedback; growth and development; interviews; motivation and incentives for growth; recruitment
time management, 19
transformation, 6–8

underperformers, 79–82
  loafers, 80–2
  strugglers, 80

Wall Street Journal, 47
Who: The A Method for Hiring (Smart & Street), 77
workshops, 45–6
  Anti-Conference, 46
  Lego Strategy Workshop, 46
  Pixar Storytelling Rules in Action, 45–6
  Role-Play Pitch Challenge, 46

Yeager, David, 52